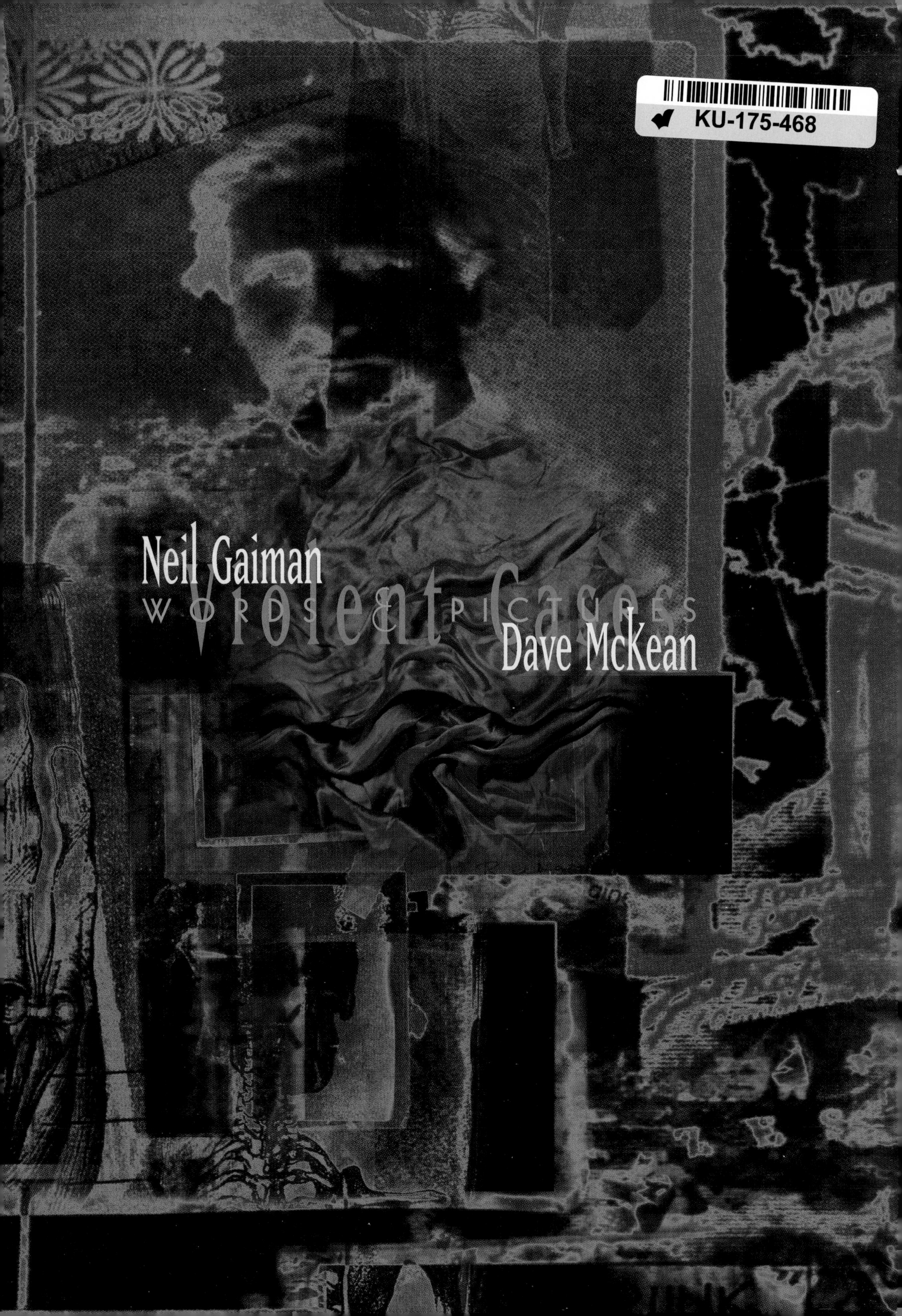
Neil Gaiman
WORDS & PICTURES
Violent Cases
Dave McKean

Dedication

For Michael, and all the other little violent cases.
—Neil Gaiman

For my teacher, Malcolm Hatton.
You see? This is what I mean by comics.
—Dave McKean

For Alan Moore. With thanks and gratitude, and,
after all these years, still a smidgen of awe.
—Neil and Dave

Violent Cases™

First Dark Horse edition: October 2003

10 9 8 7 6 5 4 3 2 1

Printed in China   ISBN 1-56971-606-4

Published by Dark Horse Books
A division of Dark Horse Comics, Inc.
10956 SE Main Street
Milwaukie, Oregon 97222
www.darkhorse.com

Mike Richardson, Publisher

INTRODUCTION by Neil Gaiman

IN 1986, I MET DAVE McKEAN.

He was still at art college. I was a young journalist. Both of us had been recruited to work for a Bright New British Anthology Comic (the title doesn't matter — it never came out, and I doubt the world has lost anything by its absence). He was drawing two strips; I was writing three other strips. Both of us had very definite ideas about the kind of comics we wanted to see, the kind of comics we liked.

They were heady times. We were both intoxicated by the potential of the medium, by the then-strange idea that comics weren't exclusively for kids anymore (if they had ever been): that the possibilities were endless.

Dave went to New York for a week and showed his portfolio to all the comics publishers he could find. They stared at him blankly and sent him home. I wrote articles for British magazines and newspapers, doing my best to tell the world about *Maus, Watchmen, Love & Rockets, Elektra: Assassin*. The Good Stuff that was out there.

In England, much of the brightest work was being showcased in *Escape*, a magazine edited by Paul Gravett. He did an article on the Bright New Anthology Comic Dave and I were working for, and liked my writing, liked Dave's art, asked if we'd be willing to work together and contribute a five-page strip to *Escape*. We agreed enthusiastically.

We talked about what we wanted to do: a comic for people who didn't read comics; something with no super-heroes, no Science Fiction, no overt genre elements; something we could show our friends, and that our friends would read, and, if we were lucky, respect.

I went away and thought.

ONE OF THE THINGS THAT HAD IMPRESSED ME MOST about the work of Dave's I'd seen so far, leaving aside his simple ability to draw the pants off most of his contemporaries, was his sense of storytelling and design. I knew that if I was going to write something for him to draw, I was going to let him tell the story, let him discover the panel progressions.

Very well. I would write the words; Dave would draw the pictures.

I finished the story — skein of words with picture-sized gaps in the text — but I didn't have a title for it. I took the story to the Milford Writers' workshop, and was told it was good, and Garry Kilworth pointed out the title to me: it was sitting in the text, wasn't it? I gave the manuscript to Dave, and he was keen to start. We went to see Paul Gravett, and explained a little hesitantly that what we were looking at doing was a 44-page graphic novel. Would he still be willing to publish it? He was. Dave did layouts, we argued about them; he requested changes in the text, we argued about them; it was great. He started to paint.

Somewhere in all that, the Bright New British Anthology Comic snuffled in pain, rolled over, and died. We hardly noticed — we were off in a world of old photographs and snippets of cloth and ivy leaves, of gangsters and osteopaths and childhood parties.

We finished it in early 1987. Alan Moore wrote an introduction, and various good people gave us quotes for the back cover. And in late 1987, it was published in the U.K. by Titan Books, in association with *Escape*. In black-and-white.

NOW LET'S FAST-FORWARD A FEW YEARS (skipping over the things that happened to Dave, myself, and *Violent Cases* in the meantime, which, in the case of the latter, include being in print continuously since it came out, being adapted into a stage play, and astonishing both of us by winning more than its fair share of awards) to the arrival of Tundra. They expressed an interest in publishing an American Edition of *Violent Cases*. Both Dave and I were excited: it had never been properly distributed in America, and only those few people who had been fortunate enough to look at Dave's original art had ever seen the wonderful chromatic range of blues and greys and browns he had introduced. This was *Violent Cases* as it was always meant to be.

And while both Dave and I have done many things since this book, together and apart, sometimes with less success, sometimes, I hope, with more, this is where it all started; this was where we began.

And while one's feelings for one's children (and, by the same token, for one's parents) must always be mixed, and while it is unwise to show favoritism, *Violent Cases* was our first child, and it commands from both of us a love and loyalty that's all its own. We're still proud of it. Especially now, dressed for a party, in its fine new colored coat.

— Neil Gaiman
Sussex, March 1991

AFTERWORD: 2003 …

I SPENT TODAY WITH DAVE McKEAN, MORE OR LESS. He was in a huge blue studio, directing our first feature film, *MirrorMask*, while I walked a journalist around, and did the interviews that he was too busy to do (my part, the writing, being mostly over, after all). At one point the journalist asked how we started out, and we told him about *Violent Cases*, seventeen years ago. My daughter, Holly, who was eighteen a few days ago, asked Dave, "When did you first meet me?" and Dave thought for a moment, and said, "When I came over to your flat to take photos of Mike for *Violent Cases*. You weren't walking yet."

It's a book about time and memory, and the time has passed, and enough time that memory plays tricks on us, and the young man who lights his cigarette in the opening panels is not the middle-aged me who gave up smoking a decade ago. But he and Dave did something very fine a long time ago, and I'm still proud of them.

— Neil Gaiman
July 2003

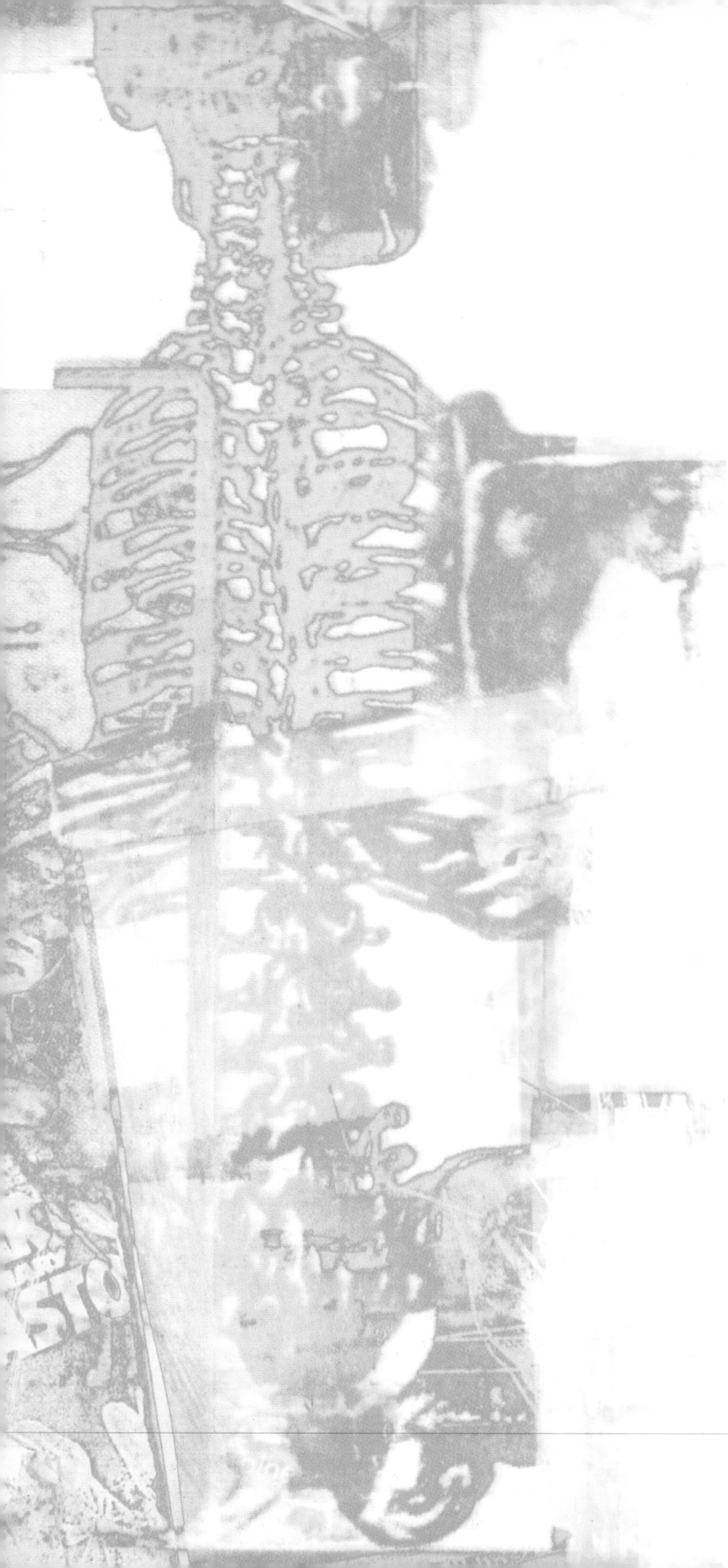

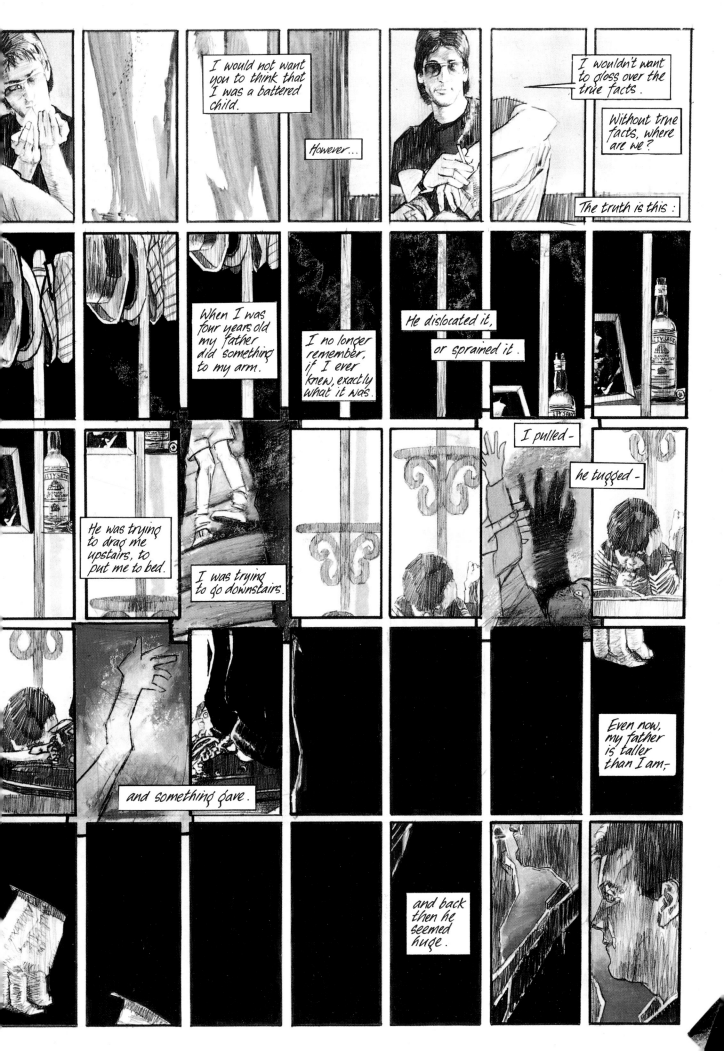

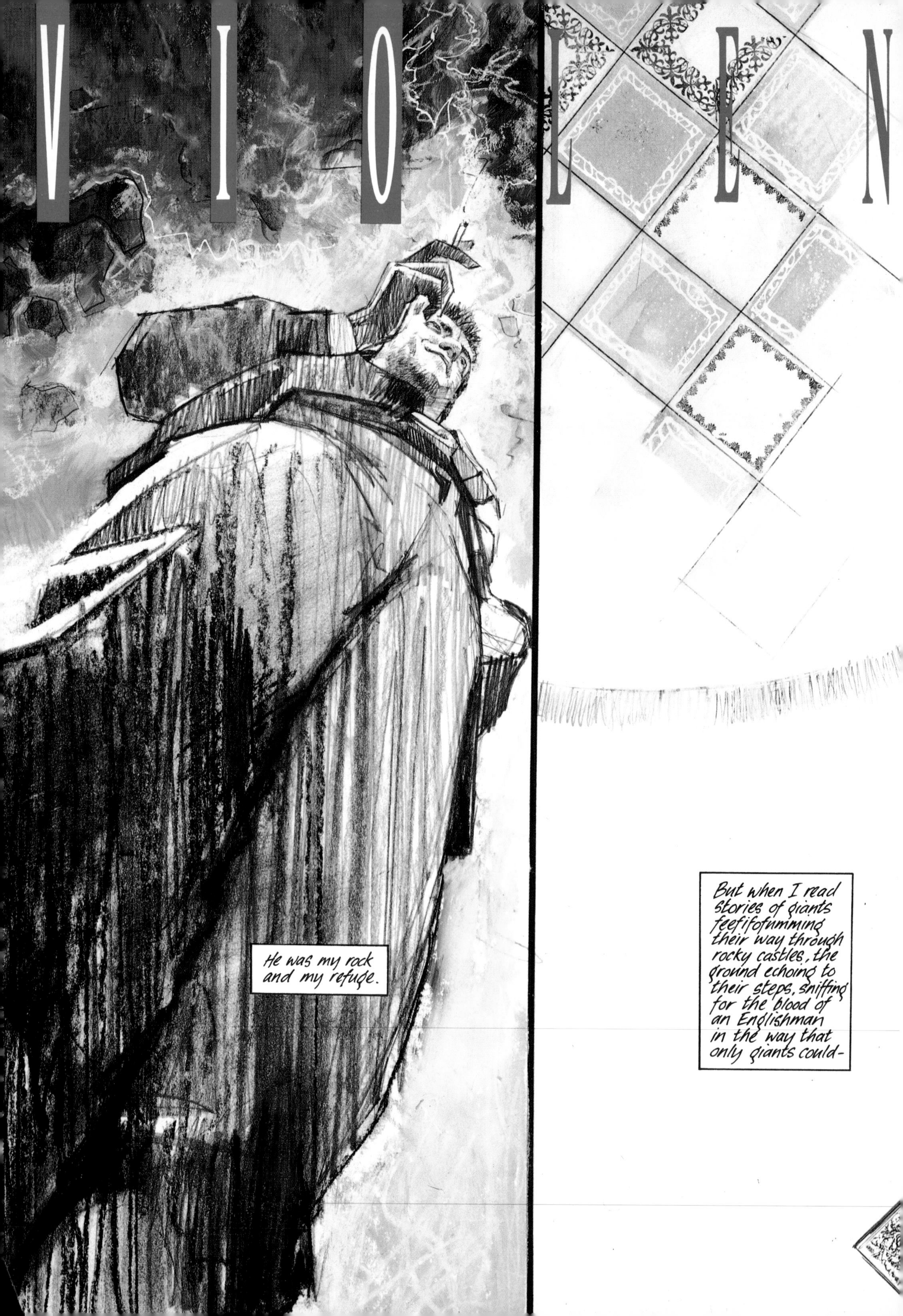
V I O L E N
He was my rock and my refuge.
But when I read stories of giants feefifofumming their way through rocky castles, the ground echoing to their steps, sniffing for the blood of an Englishman in the way that only giants could-

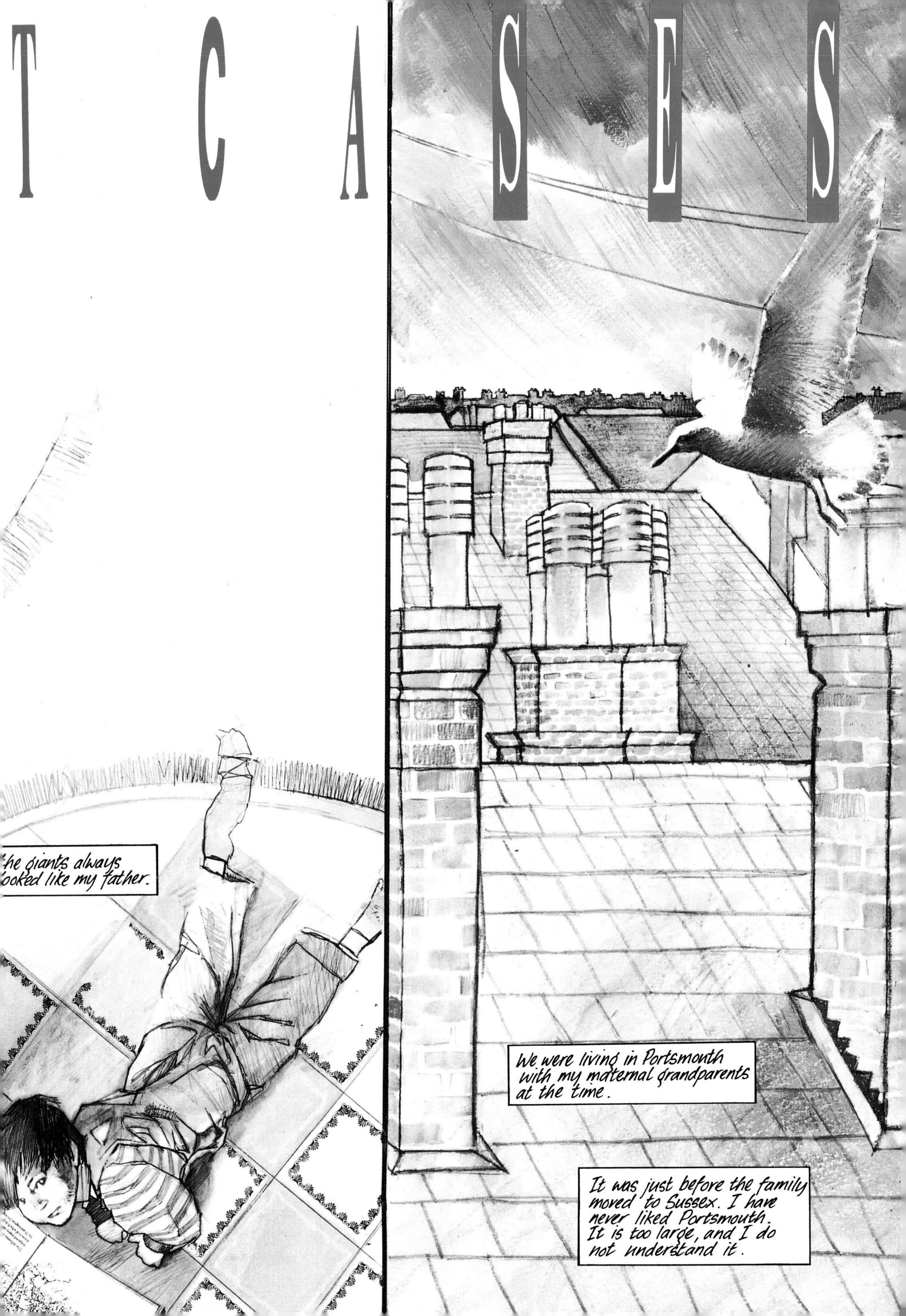
T C A S E S
he giants always
ooked like my father.
We were living in Portsmouth with my maternal grandparents at the time.
It was just before the family moved to Sussex. I have never liked Portsmouth. It is too large, and I do not understand it.

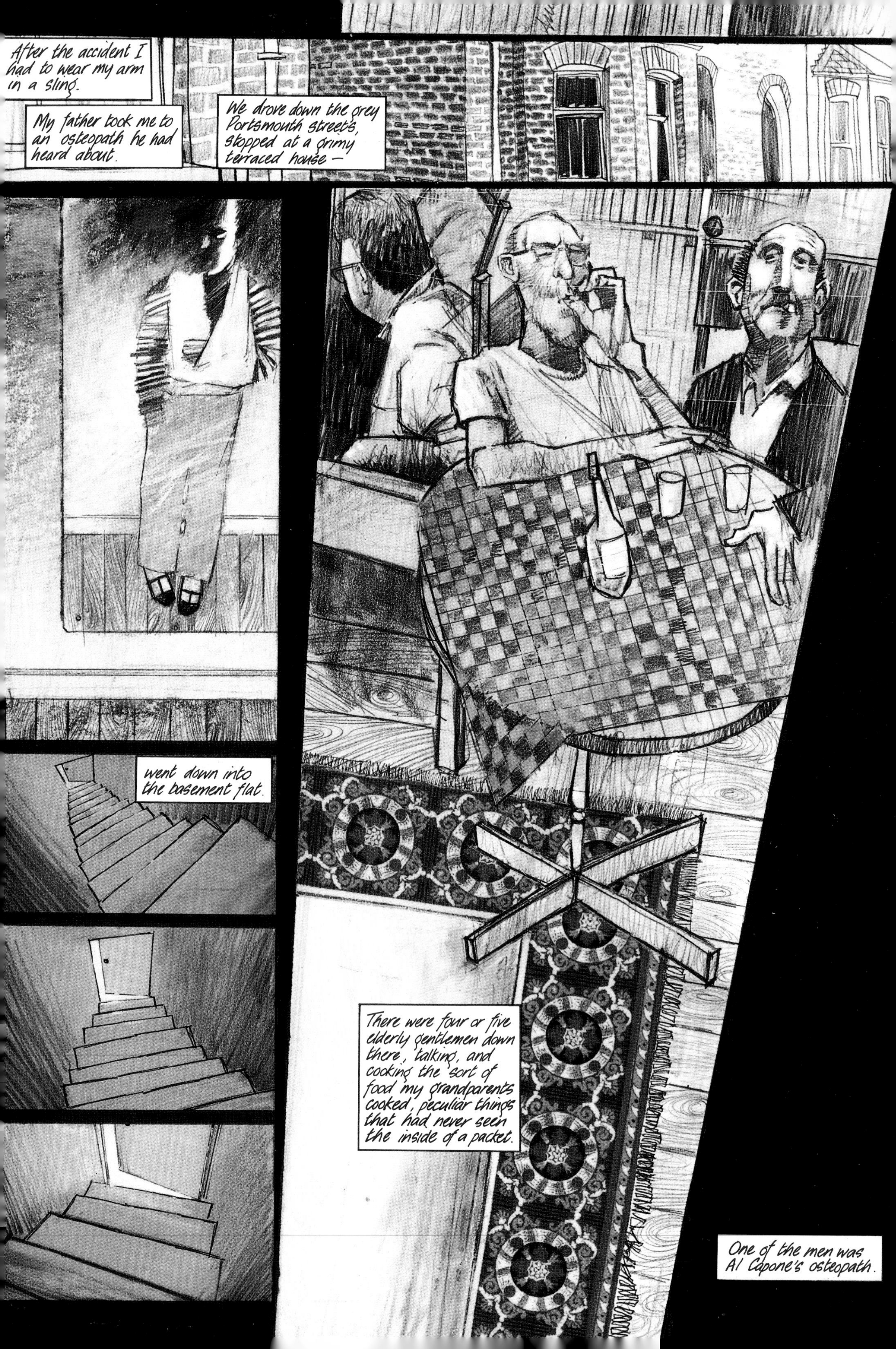
After the accident I had to wear my arm in a sling.
My father took me to an osteopath he had heard about.
We drove down the grey Portsmouth streets, stopped at a grimy terraced house —
went down into the basement flat.
There were four or five elderly gentlemen down there, talking, and cooking the sort of food my grandparents cooked, peculiar things that had never seen the inside of a packet.
One of the men was Al Capone's osteopath.

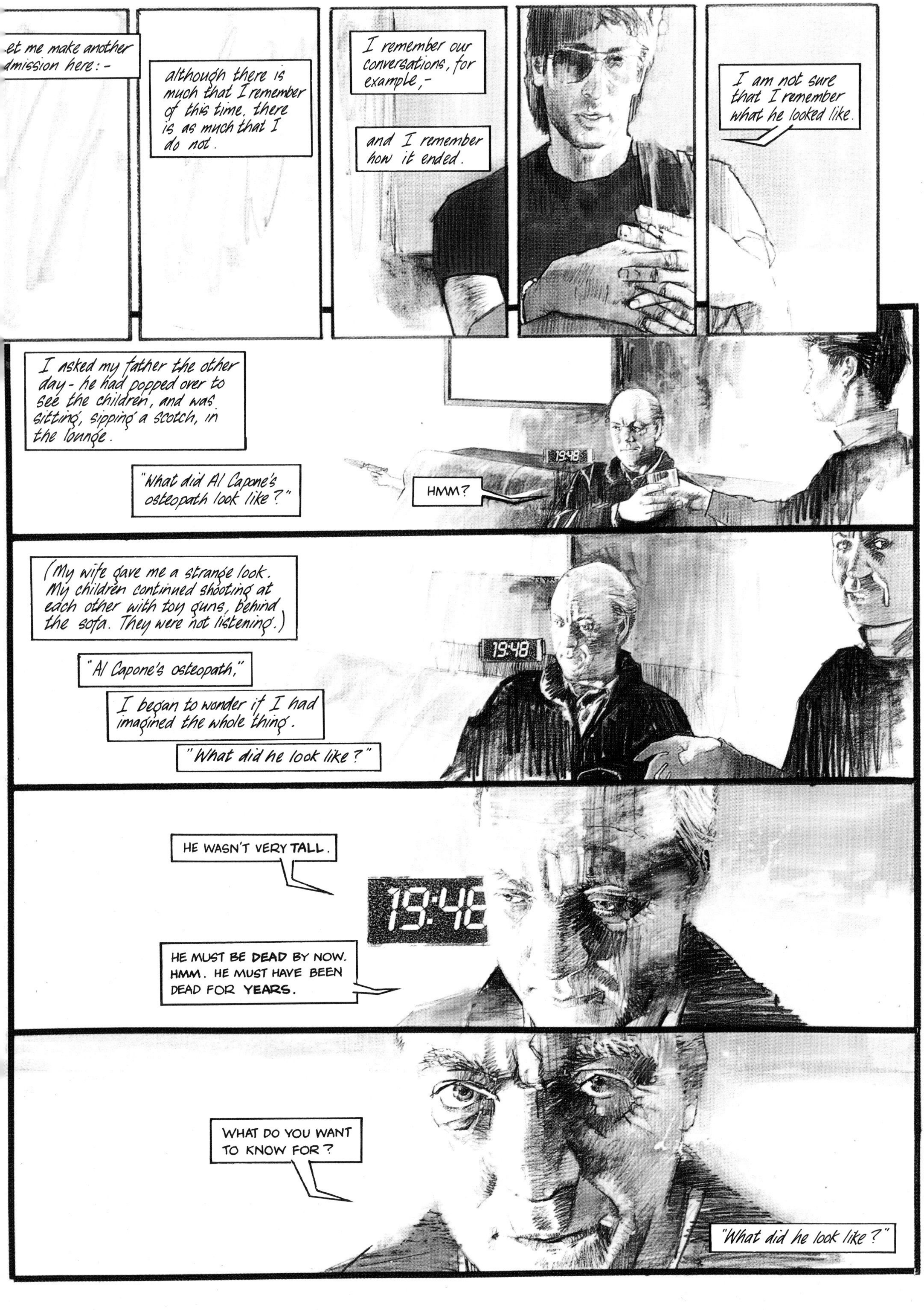
.et me make another
dmission here:-
although there is much that I remember of this time, there is as much that I do not.
I remember our conversations, for example,-
and I remember how it ended.
I am not sure that I remember what he looked like.
I asked my father the other day- he had popped over to see the children, and was sitting, sipping a scotch, in the lounge.
19:48
"What did Al Capone's osteopath look like?"
HMM?
(My wife gave me a strange look. My children continued shooting at each other with toy guns, behind the sofa. They were not listening.)
19:48
"Al Capone's osteopath,"
I began to wonder if I had imagined the whole thing.
"What did he look like?"
HE WASN'T VERY TALL.
HE MUST BE DEAD BY NOW. HMM. HE MUST HAVE BEEN DEAD FOR YEARS.
WHAT DO YOU WANT TO KNOW FOR?
"What did he look like?"

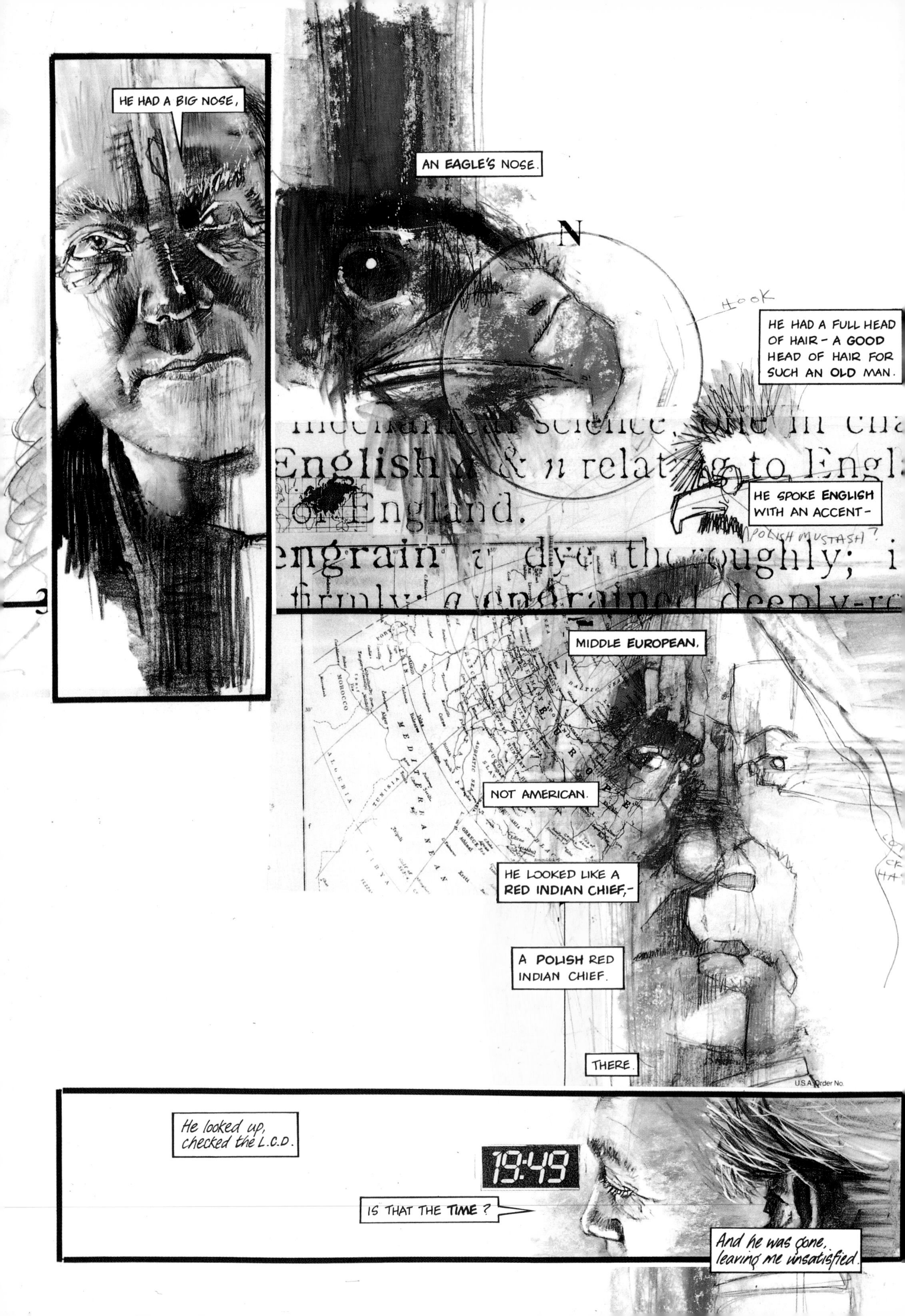

HE HAD A BIG NOSE,
AN EAGLE'S NOSE.
N
HOOK
HE HAD A FULL HEAD OF HAIR - A GOOD HEAD OF HAIR FOR SUCH AN OLD MAN.
English a & n relating to England
or England.
engrain a dye thoroughly;
HE SPOKE ENGLISH WITH AN ACCENT -
POLISH MUSTASH?
MIDDLE EUROPEAN.
NOT AMERICAN.
HE LOOKED LIKE A RED INDIAN CHIEF, -
A POLISH RED INDIAN CHIEF.
THERE.
U.S.A. Order No.
He looked up, checked the L.C.D.
19:49
IS THAT THE TIME ?
And he was gone, leaving me unsatisfied.

I am not sure that his description agrees with my own memories.

Yet my memories are blurred, vaseline-filtered :

I remember an owl-like man, chubby and friendly, —

peering at me over thick spectacles while he inspected my back and arm.

Who was this?

Not the gaunt grey chief of my father's description.

A doctor perhaps, —

or no-one at all:

I synthesise the two pictures into a third, undoubtedly imaginary.

I was four and a half.

We were alone in the consulting room. The osteopath took off my jumper and examined my arm and shoulder.

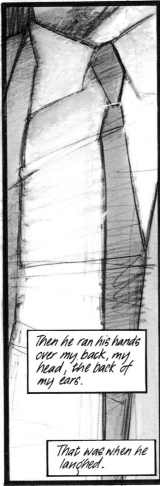

Then he ran his hands over my back, my head, the back of my ears.

That was when he laughed.

GOUT!

FEEL THESE LITTLE NODULES BEHIND YOUR EARS?

YOU GET THEM FROM GOUT!

FROM TOO MUCH PORT!

He thought this incredibly funny.

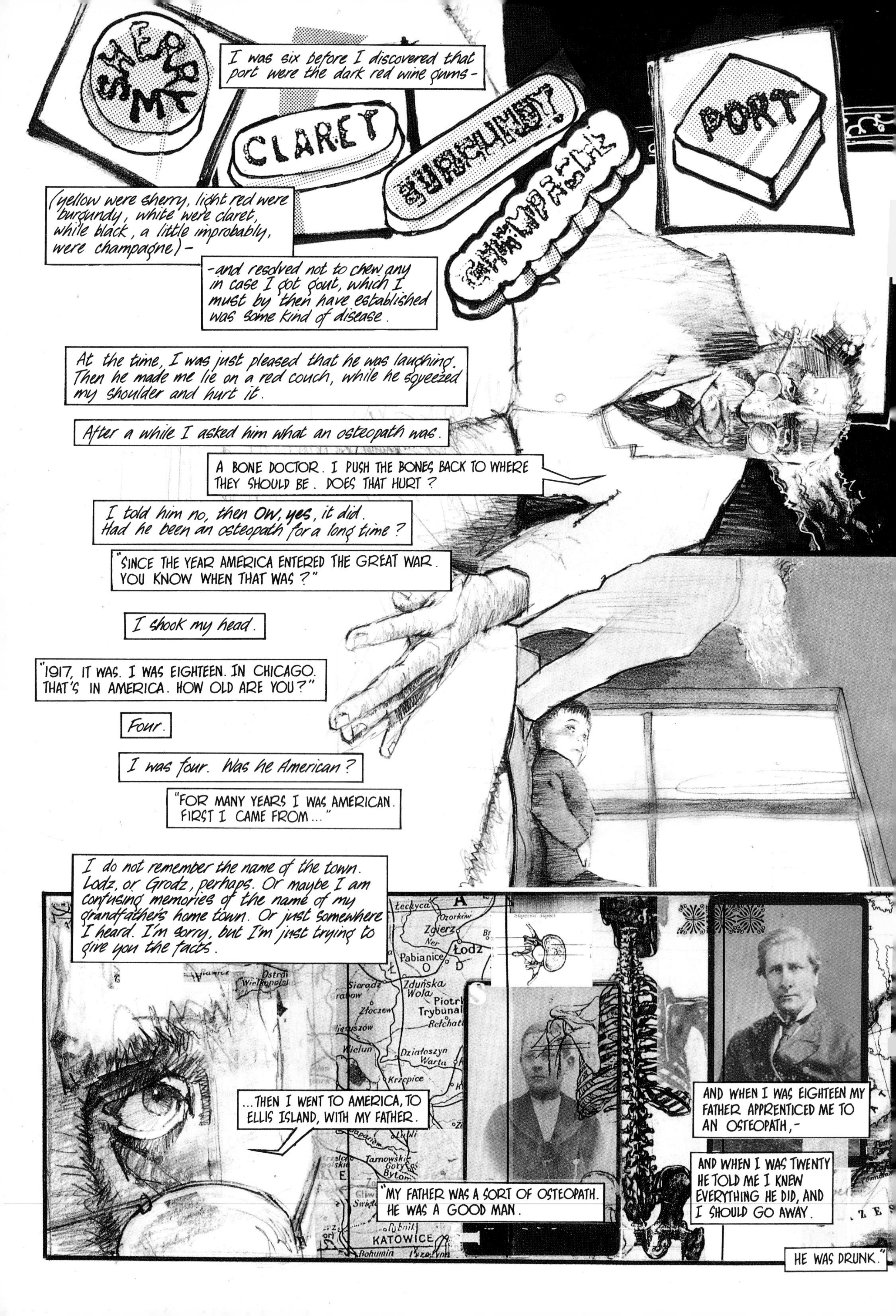

I was six before I discovered that port were the dark red wine gums -
CLARET
PORT
(yellow were sherry, light red were burgundy, white were claret, while black, a little improbably, were champagne) -
-and resolved not to chew any in case I got gout, which I must by then have established was some kind of disease.
At the time, I was just pleased that he was laughing. Then he made me lie on a red couch, while he squeezed my shoulder and hurt it.
After a while I asked him what an osteopath was.
A BONE DOCTOR. I PUSH THE BONES BACK TO WHERE THEY SHOULD BE. DOES THAT HURT?
I told him no, then OW, yes, it did. Had he been an osteopath for a long time?
"SINCE THE YEAR AMERICA ENTERED THE GREAT WAR. YOU KNOW WHEN THAT WAS?"
I shook my head.
"1917, IT WAS. I WAS EIGHTEEN. IN CHICAGO. THAT'S IN AMERICA. HOW OLD ARE YOU?"
Four.
I was four. Was he American?
"FOR MANY YEARS I WAS AMERICAN. FIRST I CAME FROM..."
I do not remember the name of the town. Lodz, or Grodz, perhaps. Or maybe I am confusing memories of the name of my grandfather's home town. Or just somewhere I heard. I'm sorry, but I'm just trying to give you the facts.
Zgierz
Łodz
Pabianice
Sieradz
Zduńska Wola
Złoczew
Trybunal
Bełchatów
Wieluń
Działoszyn
Warta
Krzepice
Superior aspect
...THEN I WENT TO AMERICA, TO ELLIS ISLAND, WITH MY FATHER.
"MY FATHER WAS A SORT OF OSTEOPATH. HE WAS A GOOD MAN.
AND WHEN I WAS EIGHTEEN MY FATHER APPRENTICED ME TO AN OSTEOPATH, -
AND WHEN I WAS TWENTY HE TOLD ME I KNEW EVERYTHING HE DID, AND I SHOULD GO AWAY.
KATOWICE
HE WAS DRUNK."

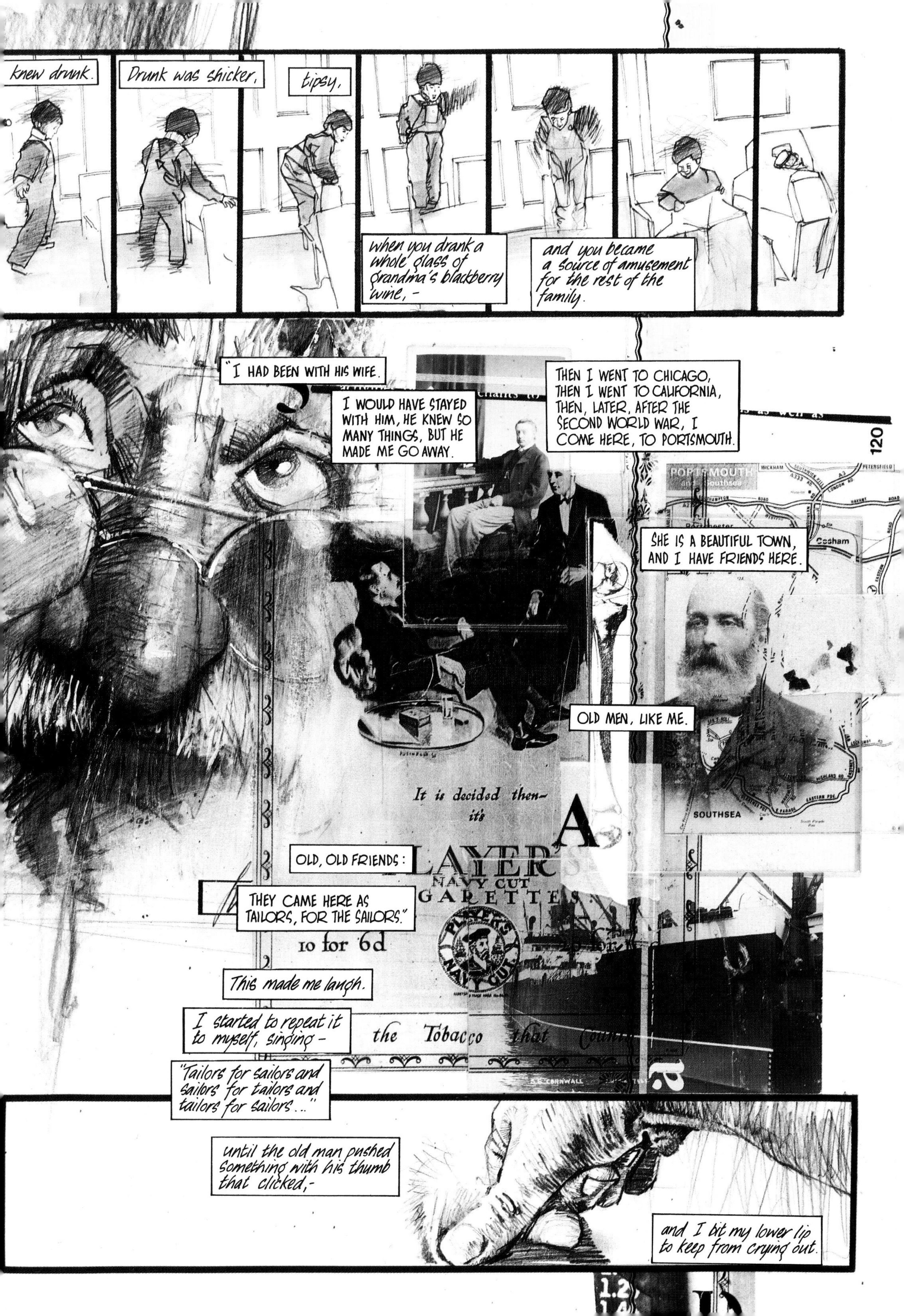

knew drunk.
Drunk was shicker,
tipsy,
when you drank a whole glass of grandma's blackberry wine, -
and you became a source of amusement for the rest of the family.
"I HAD BEEN WITH HIS WIFE.
I WOULD HAVE STAYED WITH HIM, HE KNEW SO MANY THINGS, BUT HE MADE ME GO AWAY.
THEN I WENT TO CHICAGO, THEN I WENT TO CALIFORNIA, THEN, LATER, AFTER THE SECOND WORLD WAR, I COME HERE, TO PORTSMOUTH.
SHE IS A BEAUTIFUL TOWN, AND I HAVE FRIENDS HERE.
OLD MEN, LIKE ME.
OLD, OLD FRIENDS:
THEY CAME HERE AS TAILORS, FOR THE SAILORS."
It is decided then-
it's
NAVY CUT
10 for 6d
the Tobacco
PORTSMOUTH
Cosham
SOUTHSEA
This made me laugh.
I started to repeat it to myself, singing -
"Tailors for sailors and sailors for tailors and tailors for sailors..."
until the old man pushed something with his thumb that clicked, -
and I bit my lower lip to keep from crying out.

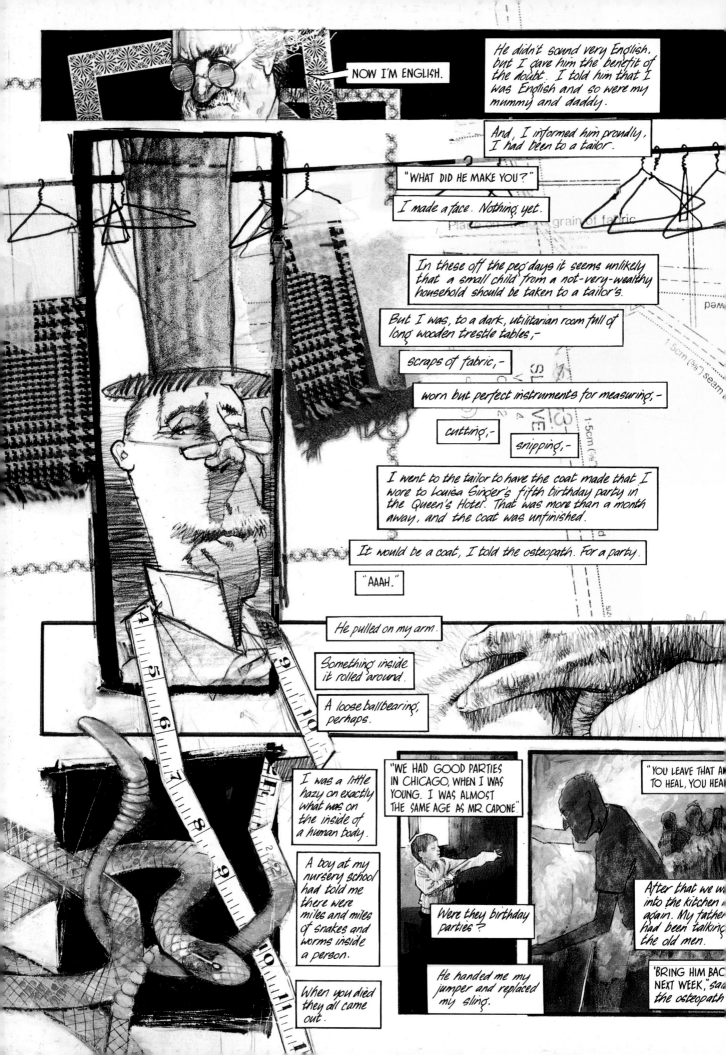

NOW I'M ENGLISH.

He didn't sound very English, but I gave him the benefit of the doubt. I told him that I was English and so were my mummy and daddy.

And, I informed him proudly, I had been to a tailor.

"WHAT DID HE MAKE YOU?"

I made a face. Nothing, yet.

In these off the peg days it seems unlikely that a small child from a not-very-wealthy household should be taken to a tailor's.

But I was, to a dark, utilitarian room full of long wooden trestle tables,—

scraps of fabric,—

worn but perfect instruments for measuring,—

cutting,—

snipping,—

I went to the tailor to have the coat made that I wore to Louisa Singer's fifth birthday party in the Queen's Hotel. That was more than a month away, and the coat was unfinished.

It would be a coat, I told the osteopath. For a party.

"AAAH."

He pulled on my arm.

Something inside it rolled around.

A loose ballbearing, perhaps.

I was a little hazy on exactly what was on the inside of a human body.

A boy at my nursery school had told me there were miles and miles of snakes and worms inside a person.

When you died they all came out.

"WE HAD GOOD PARTIES IN CHICAGO, WHEN I WAS YOUNG. I WAS ALMOST THE SAME AGE AS MR. CAPONE."

Were they birthday parties?

He handed me my jumper and replaced my sling.

"YOU LEAVE THAT A TO HEAL, YOU HEA

After that we w into the kitchen again. My father had been talking the old men.

"BRING HIM BAC NEXT WEEK," sai the osteopath

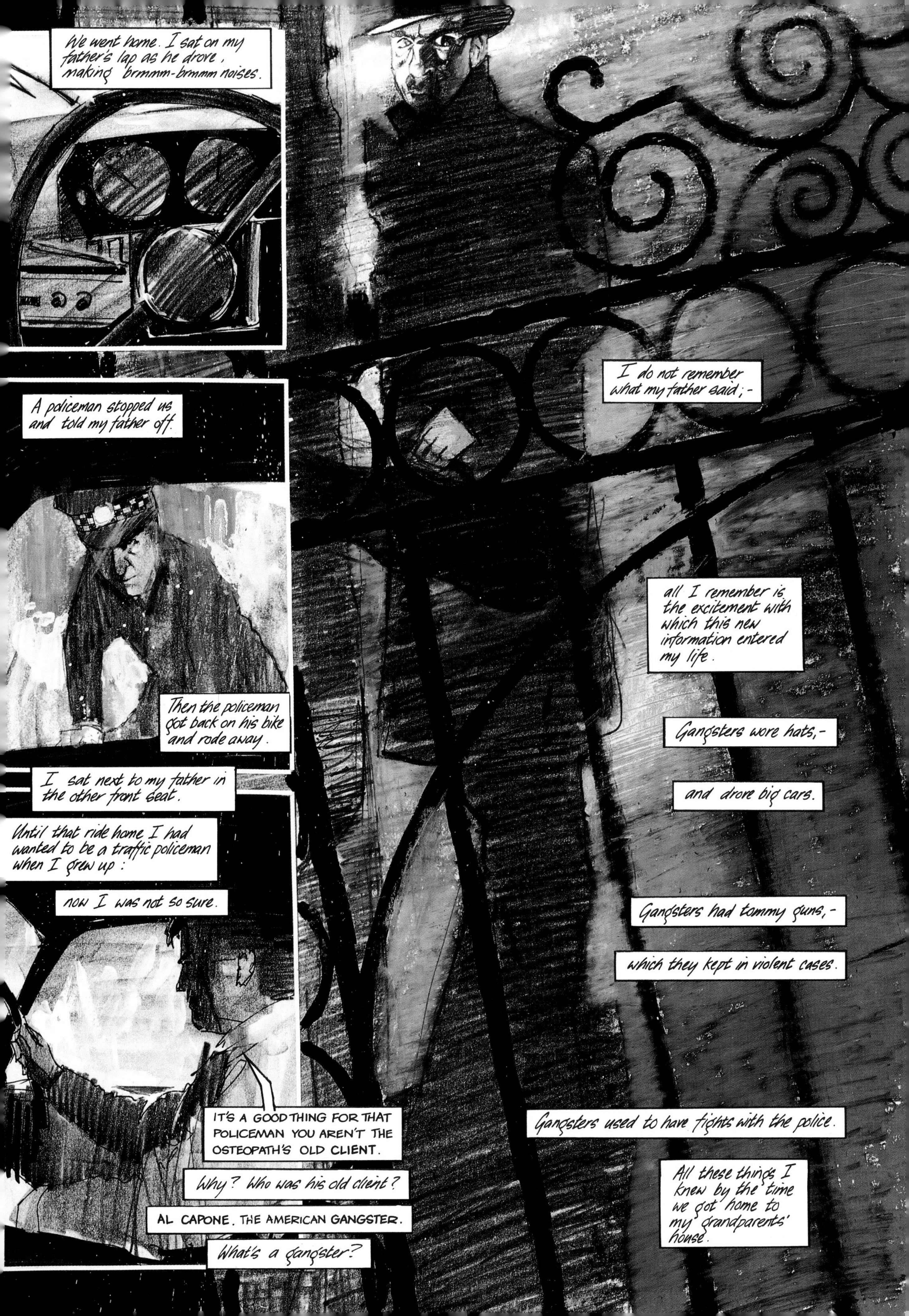

We went home. I sat on my father's lap as he drove, making brmmm-brmmm noises.
A policeman stopped us and told my father off.
Then the policeman got back on his bike and rode away.
I sat next to my father in the other front seat.
Until that ride home I had wanted to be a traffic policeman when I grew up:
now I was not so sure.
IT'S A GOOD THING FOR THAT POLICEMAN YOU AREN'T THE OSTEOPATH'S OLD CLIENT.
Why? Who was his old client?
AL CAPONE. THE AMERICAN GANGSTER.
What's a gangster?
I do not remember what my father said;-
all I remember is the excitement with which this new information entered my life.
Gangsters wore hats,-
and drove big cars.
Gangsters had tommy guns,-
which they kept in violent cases.
Gangsters used to have fights with the police.
All these things I knew by the time we got home to my grandparents' house.

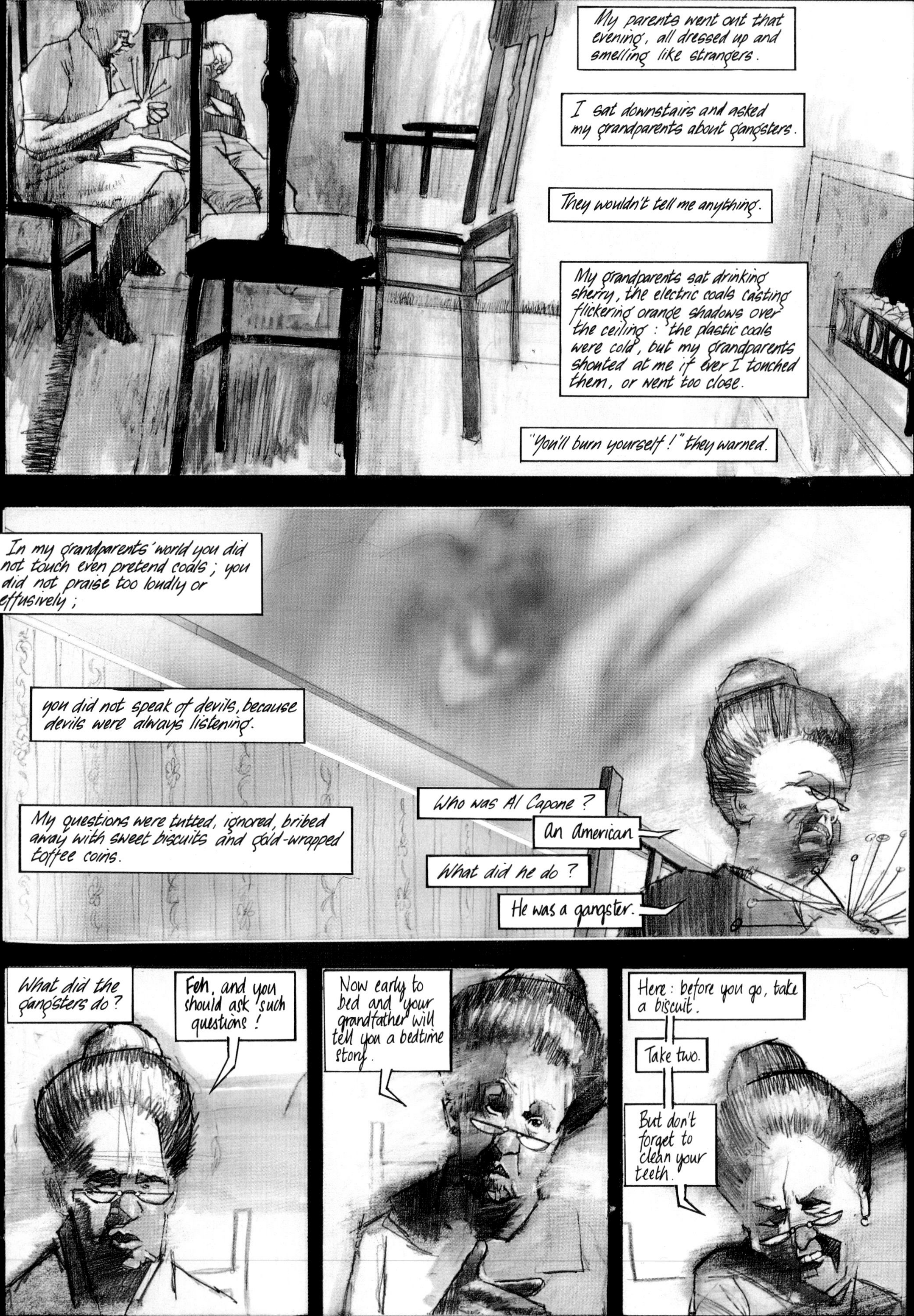

My parents went out that evening, all dressed up and smelling like strangers.
I sat downstairs and asked my grandparents about gangsters.
They wouldn't tell me anything.
My grandparents sat drinking sherry, the electric coals casting flickering orange shadows over the ceiling: the plastic coals were cold, but my grandparents shouted at me if ever I touched them, or went too close.
"You'll burn yourself!" they warned.
In my grandparents' world you did not touch even pretend coals; you did not praise too loudly or effusively;
you did not speak of devils, because devils were always listening.
My questions were tutted, ignored, bribed away with sweet biscuits and gold-wrapped toffee coins.
Who was Al Capone?
An American.
What did he do?
He was a gangster.
What did the gangsters do?
Feh, and you should ask such questions!
Now early to bed and your grandfather will tell you a bedtime story.
Here: before you go, take a biscuit.
Take two.
But don't forget to clean your teeth.

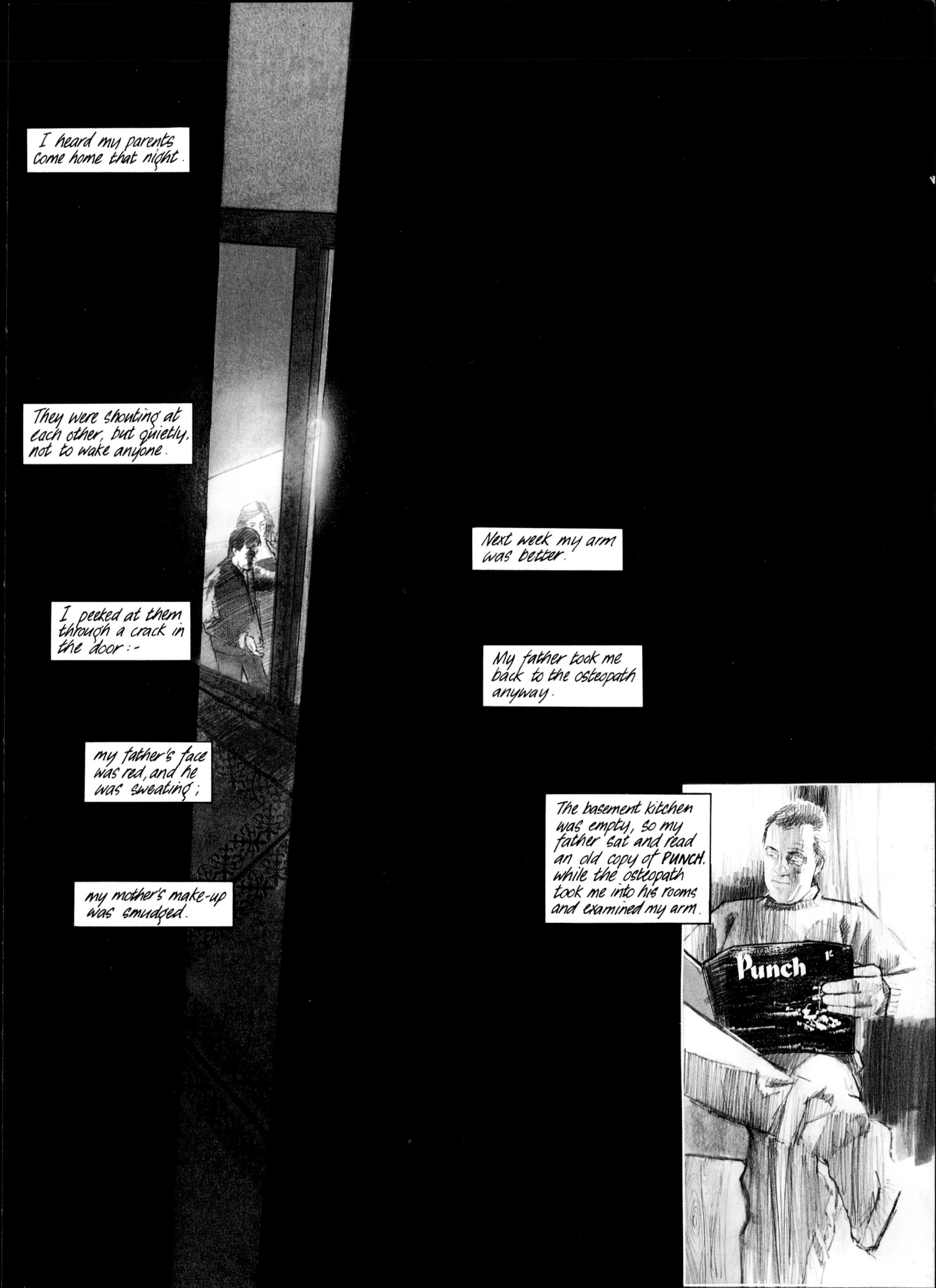
I heard my parents come home that night.
They were shouting at each other, but quietly, not to wake anyone.
I peeked at them through a crack in the door:-
my father's face was red, and he was sweating;
my mother's make-up was smudged.
Next week my arm was better.
My father took me back to the osteopath anyway.
The basement kitchen was empty, so my father sat and read an old copy of PUNCH, while the osteopath took me into his rooms and examined my arm.
Punch

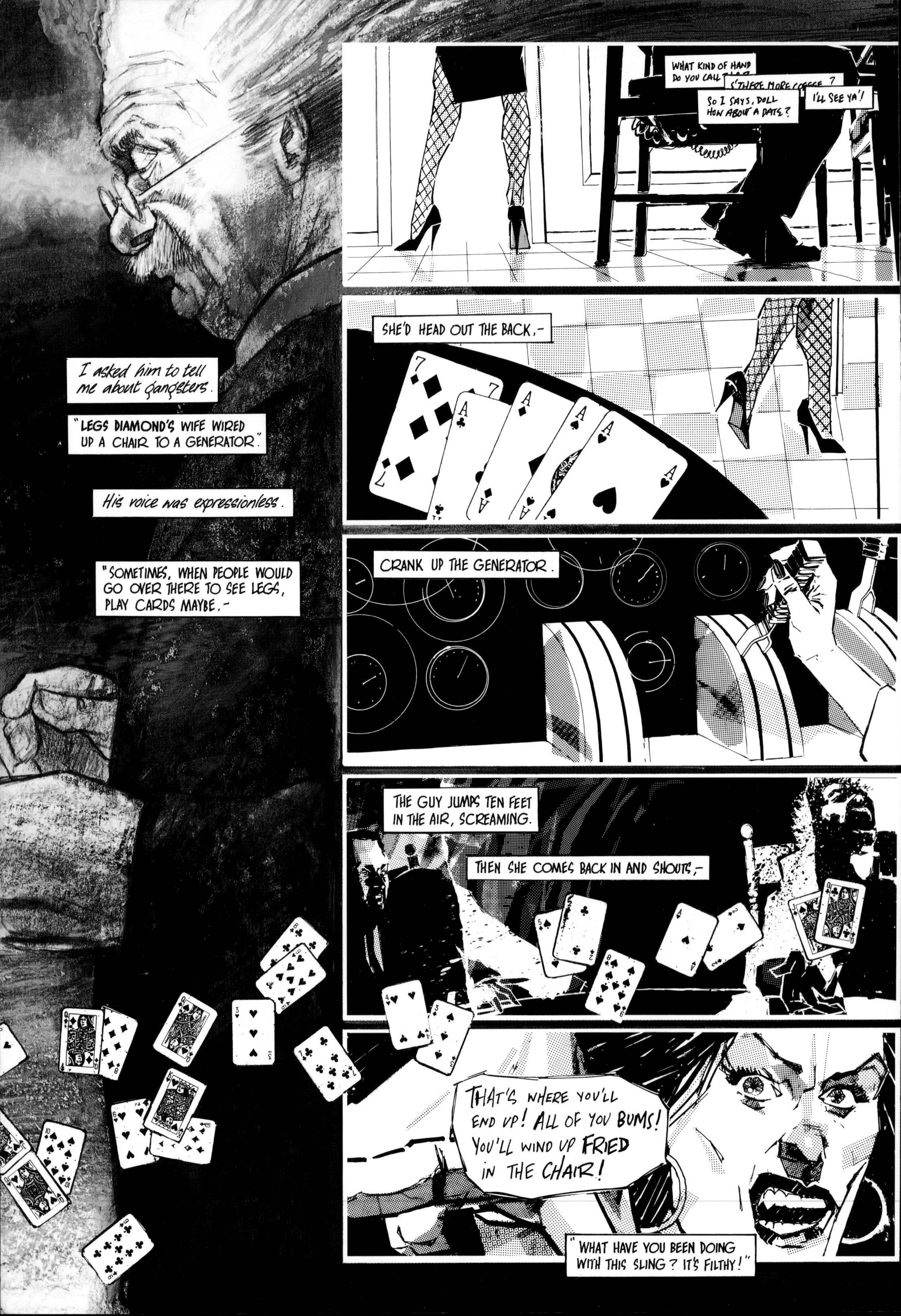
I asked him to tell me about gangsters.
"LEGS DIAMOND'S WIFE WIRED UP A CHAIR TO A GENERATOR".
His voice was expressionless.
"SOMETIMES, WHEN PEOPLE WOULD GO OVER THERE TO SEE LEGS, PLAY CARDS MAYBE.-
WHAT KIND OF HAND DO YOU CALL
S'THERE MORE CO ?
SO I SAYS, DOLL HOW ABOUT A DATE?
I'LL SEE YA'!
SHE'D HEAD OUT THE BACK,-
CRANK UP THE GENERATOR.
THE GUY JUMPS TEN FEET IN THE AIR, SCREAMING.
THEN SHE COMES BACK IN AND SHOUTS,-
THAT'S WHERE YOU'LL END UP! ALL OF YOU BUMS! YOU'LL WIND UP FRIED IN THE CHAIR!
"WHAT HAVE YOU BEEN DOING WITH THIS SLING? IT'S FILTHY!"

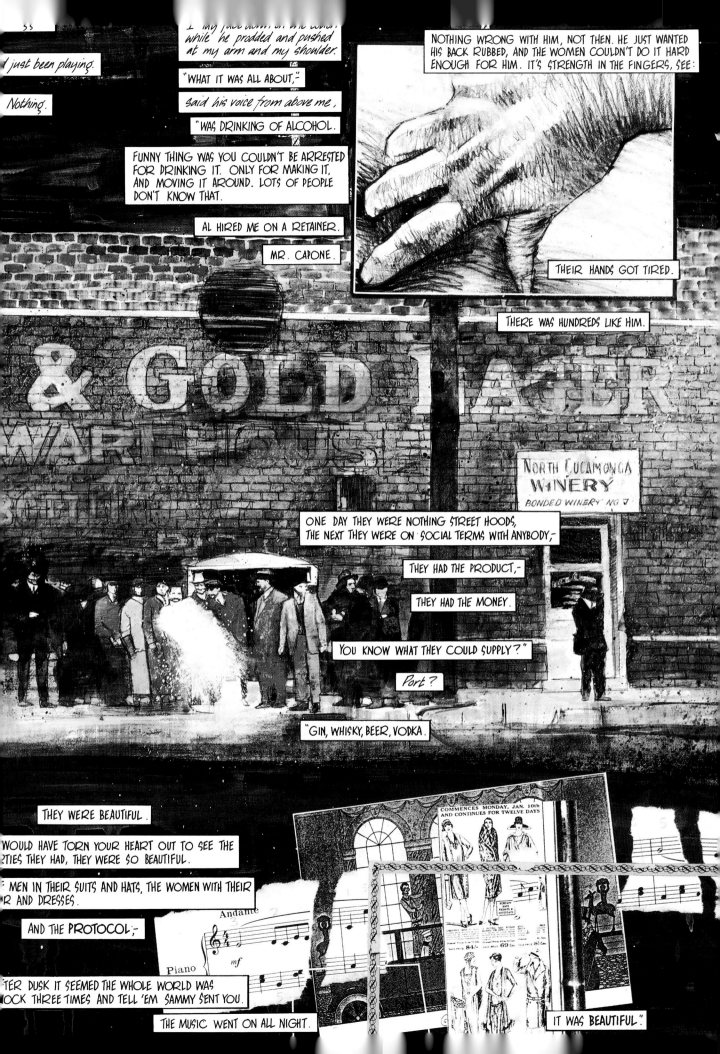

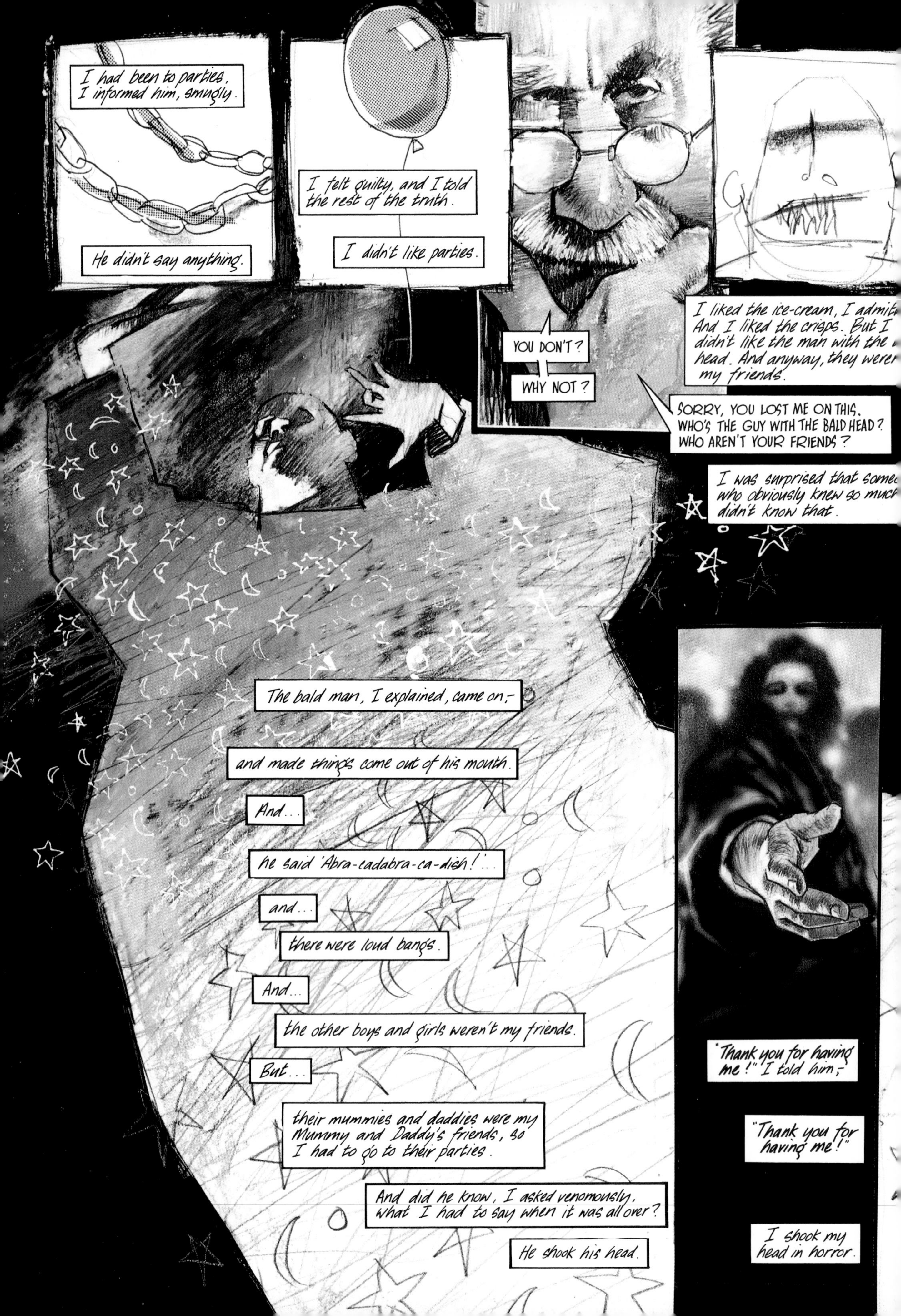

I had been to parties, I informed him, smugly.
He didn't say anything.
I felt guilty, and I told the rest of the truth.
I didn't like parties.
YOU DON'T?
WHY NOT?
I liked the ice-cream, I admit
And I liked the crisps. But I didn't like the man with the
head. And anyway, they were
my friends.
SORRY, YOU LOST ME ON THIS. WHO'S THE GUY WITH THE BALD HEAD? WHO AREN'T YOUR FRIENDS?
I was surprised that some
who obviously knew so much
didn't know that.
The bald man, I explained, came on;-
and made things come out of his mouth.
And...
he said 'Abra-cadabra-ca-dish!'...
and...
there were loud bangs.
And...
the other boys and girls weren't my friends.
But...
their mummies and daddies were my Mummy and Daddy's friends, so I had to go to their parties.
And did he know, I asked venomously, what I had to say when it was all over?
He shook his head.
"Thank you for having me!" I told him;-
"Thank you for having me!"
I shook my head in horror.

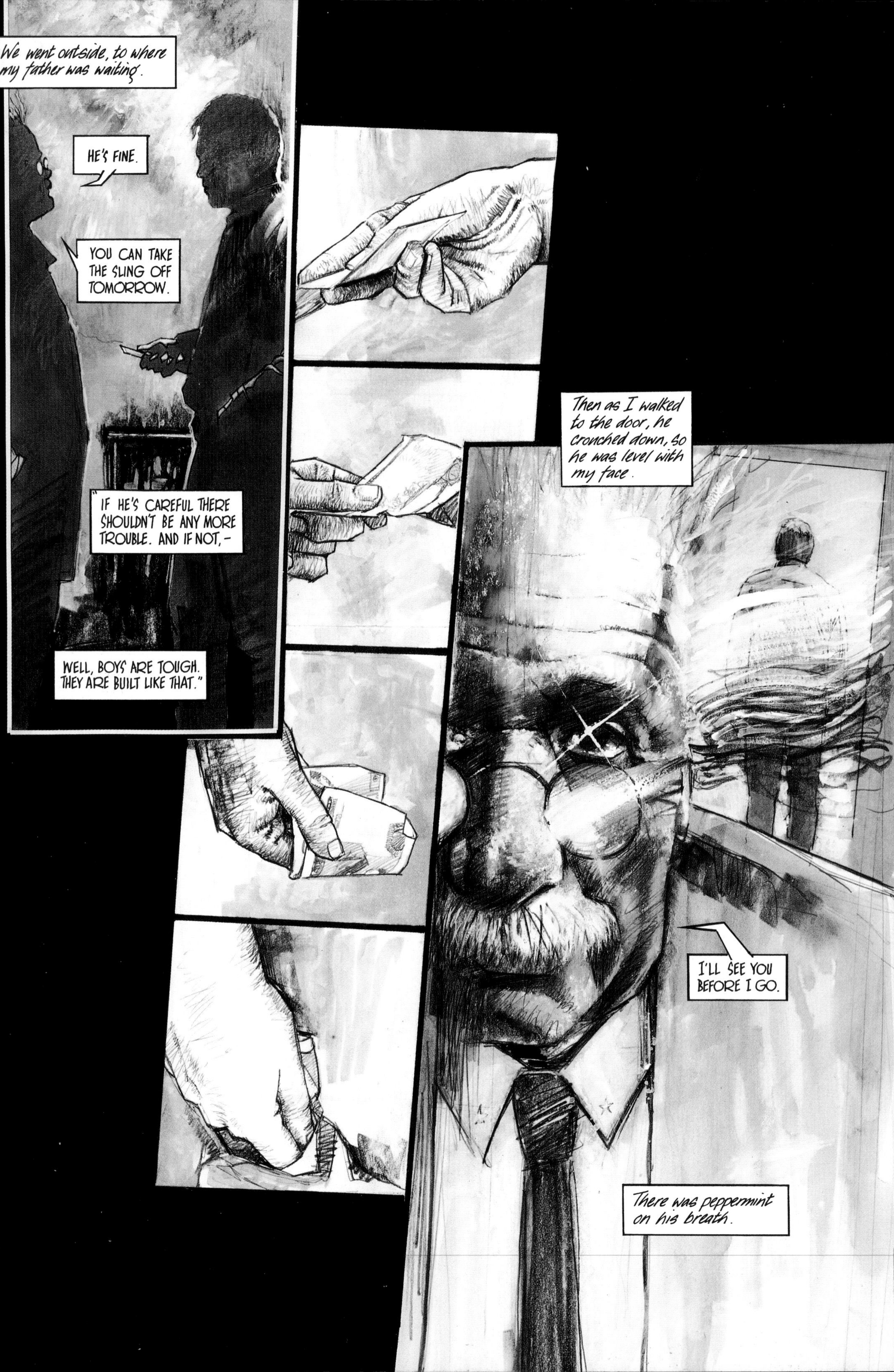
We went outside, to where my father was waiting.
HE'S FINE.
YOU CAN TAKE THE SLING OFF TOMORROW.
"IF HE'S CAREFUL THERE SHOULDN'T BE ANY MORE TROUBLE. AND IF NOT, -
WELL, BOYS ARE TOUGH. THEY ARE BUILT LIKE THAT."
Then as I walked to the door, he crouched down, so he was level with my face.
I'LL SEE YOU BEFORE I GO.
There was peppermint on his breath.

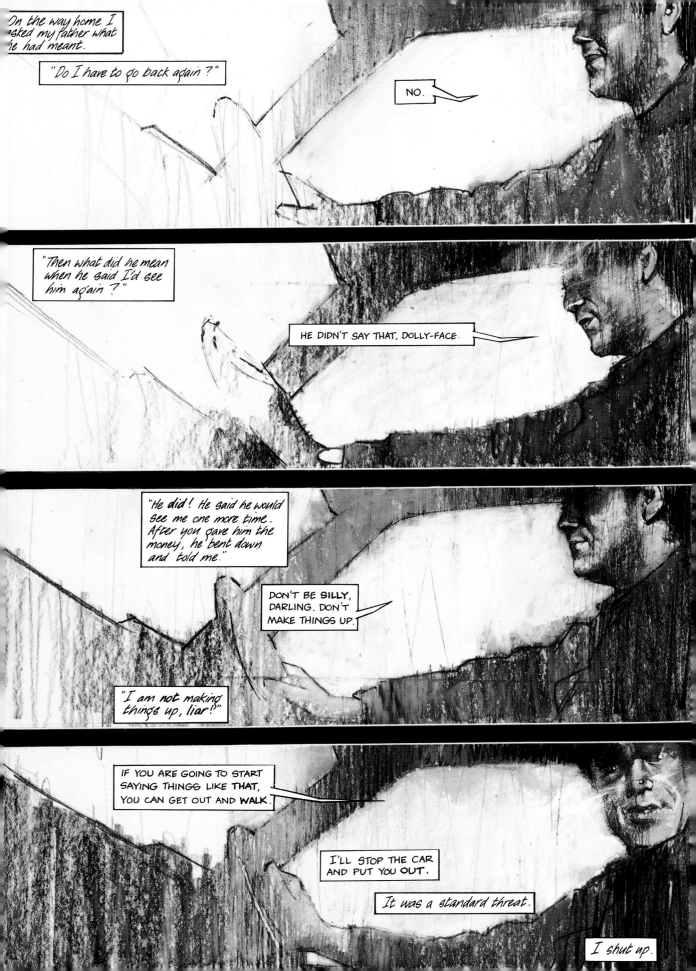

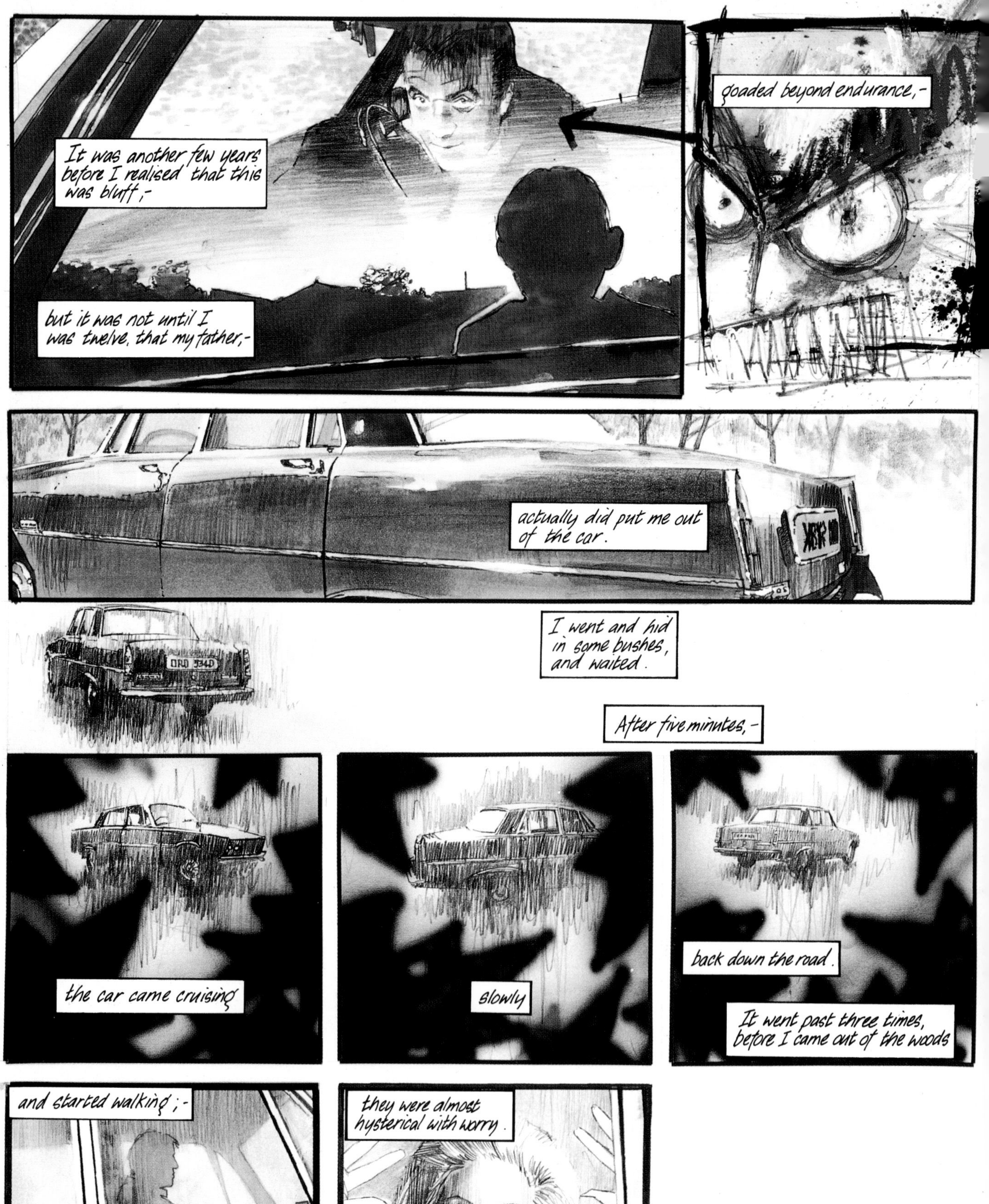
It was another few years before I realised that this was bluff,-
but it was not until I was twelve, that my father,-
goaded beyond endurance,-
actually did put me out of the car.
I went and hid in some bushes, and waited.
After five minutes,-
the car came cruising
slowly
back down the road.
It went past three times, before I came out of the woods
and started walking;-
by the time they picked me up,-
they were almost hysterical with worry.
My mother had obviously been screaming at my father.
They were very nice to me all the way home.

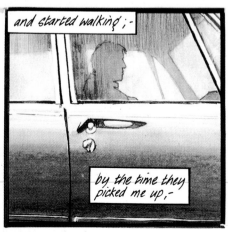

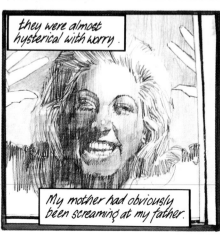

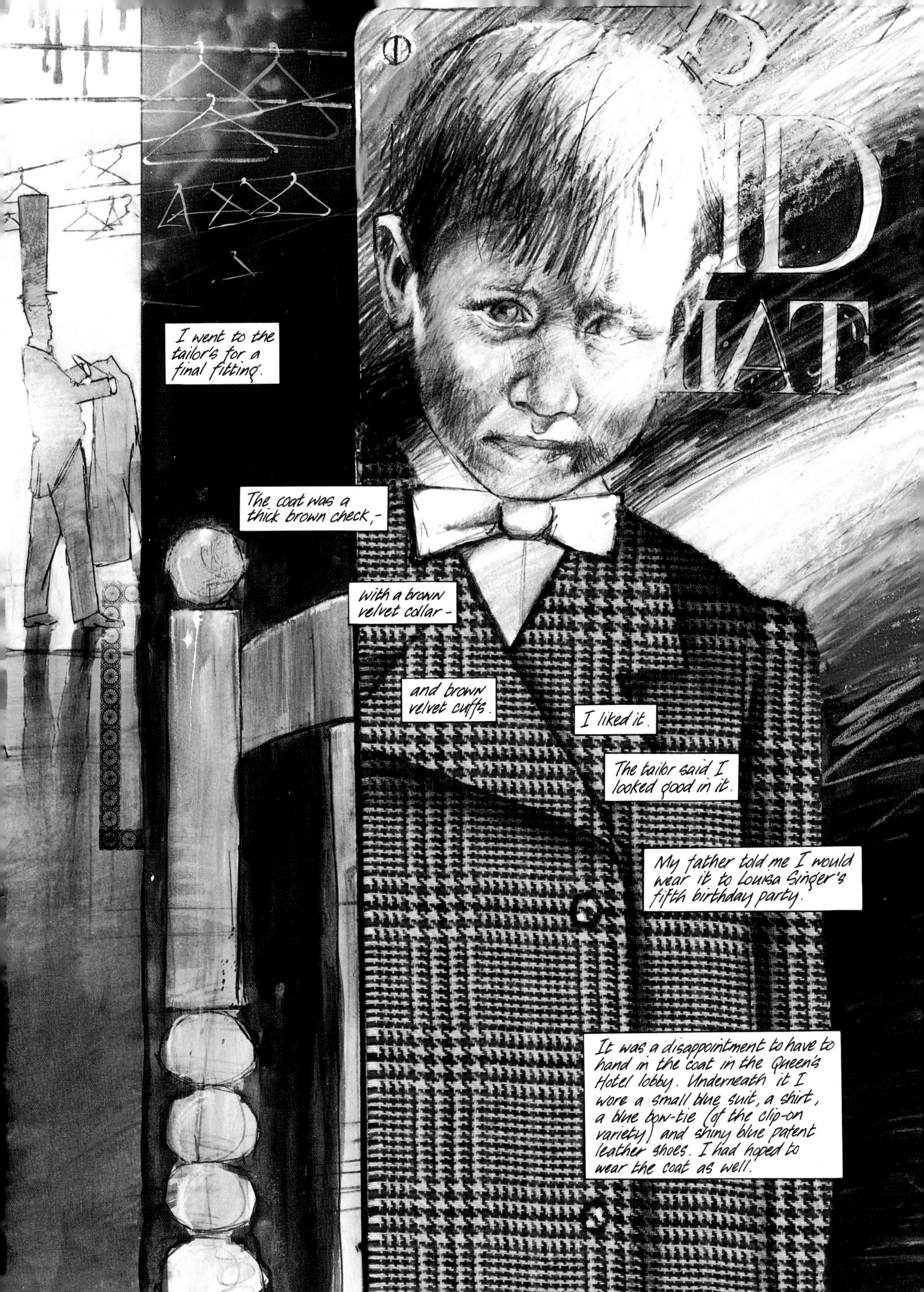

I went to the tailor's for a final fitting.
The coat was a thick brown check,-
with a brown velvet collar -
and brown velvet cuffs.
I liked it.
The tailor said I looked good in it.
My father told me I would wear it to Louisa Singer's fifth birthday party.
It was a disappointment to have to hand in the coat in the Queen's Hotel lobby. Underneath it I wore a small blue suit, a shirt, a blue bow-tie (of the clip-on variety) and shiny blue patent leather shoes. I had hoped to wear the coat as well.

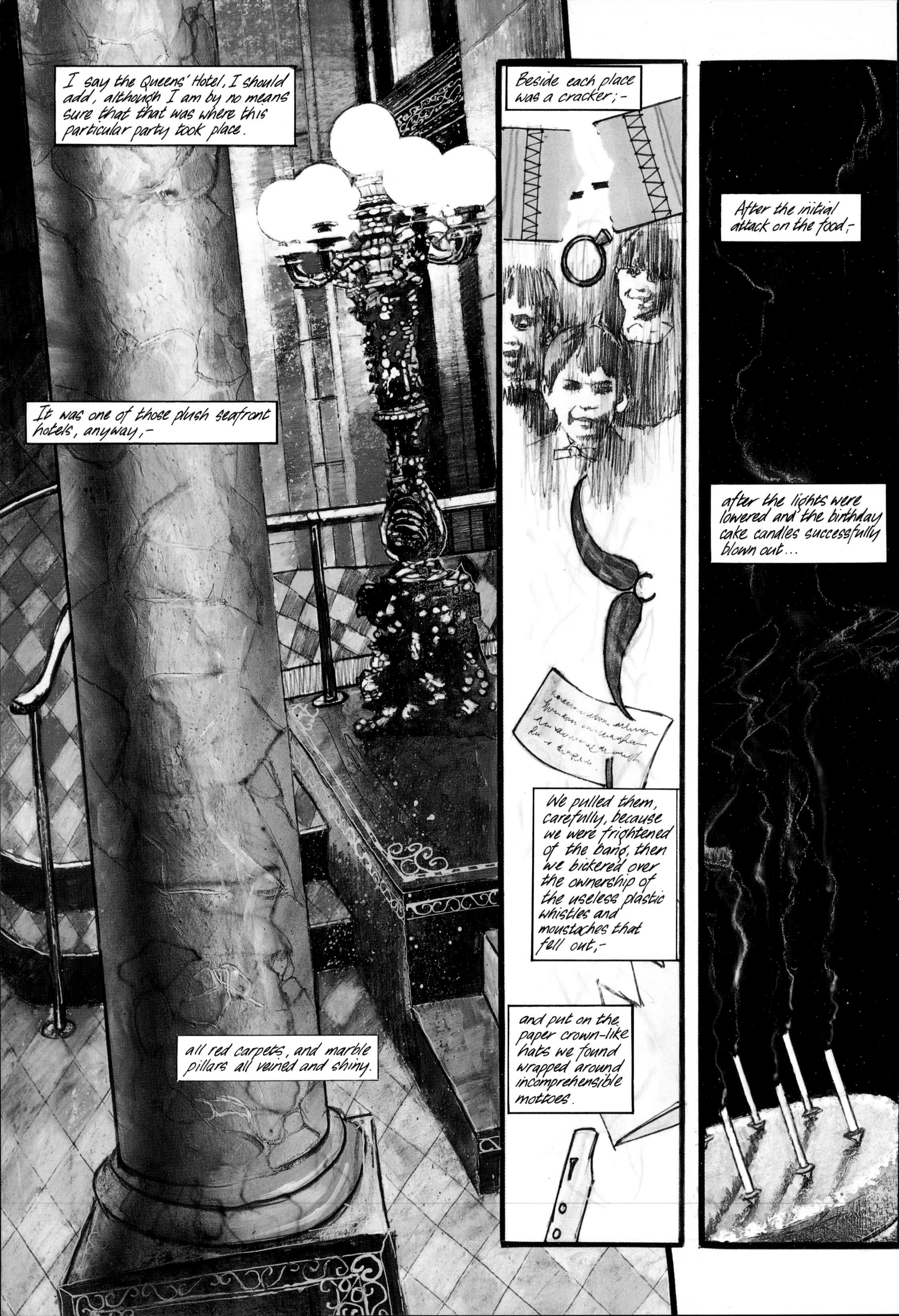
I say the Queens' Hotel, I should add, although I am by no means sure that that was where this particular party took place.
It was one of those plush seafront hotels, anyway,-
all red carpets, and marble pillars all veined and shiny.
Beside each place was a cracker;-
We pulled them, carefully, because we were frightened of the bang, then we bickered over the ownership of the useless plastic whistles and moustaches that fell out,-
and put on the paper crown-like hats we found wrapped around incomprehensible mottoes.
After the initial attack on the food,-
after the lights were lowered and the birthday cake candles successfully blown out...

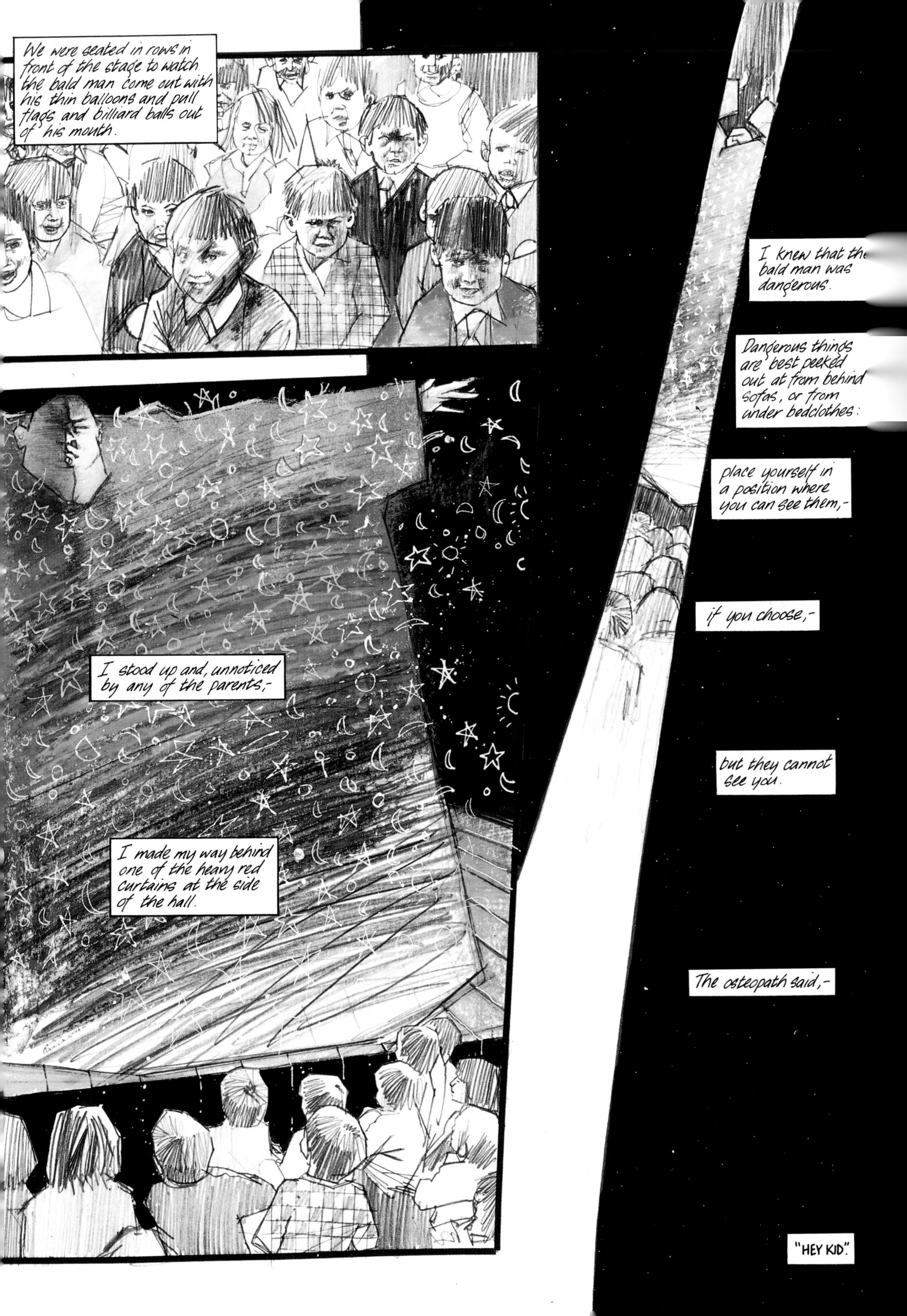
We were seated in rows in front of the stage to watch the bald man come out with his thin balloons and pull flags and billiard balls out of his month.
I knew that the bald man was dangerous.
Dangerous things are best peeked out at from behind sofas, or from under bedclothes:
place yourself in a position where you can see them,-
I stood up and, unnoticed by any of the parents,-
if you choose,-
but they cannot see you.
I made my way behind one of the heavy red curtains at the side of the hall.
The osteopath said,-
"HEY KID".

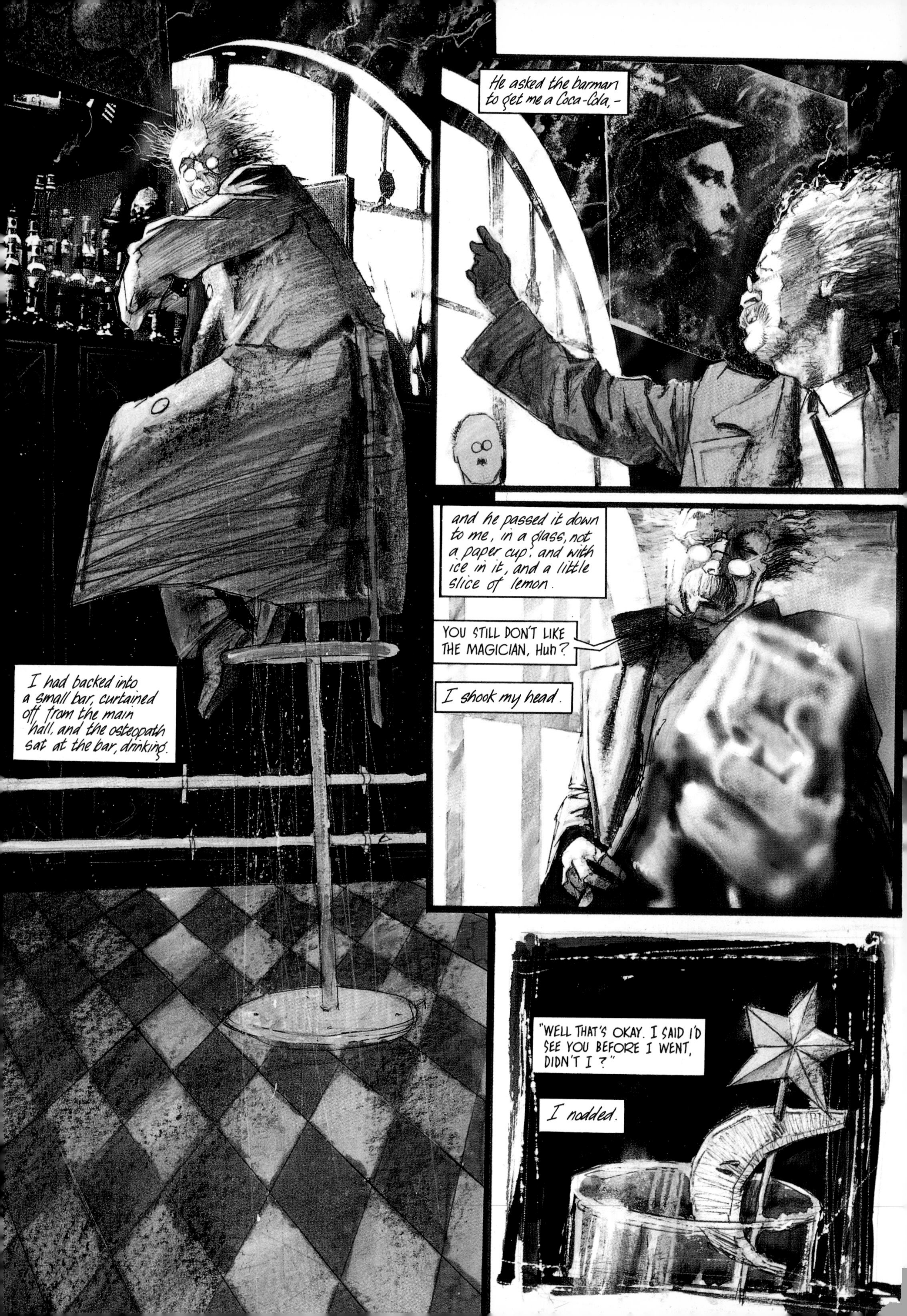
I had backed into a small bar, curtained off from the main hall, and the osteopath sat at the bar, drinking.
He asked the barman to get me a Coca-Cola, -
and he passed it down to me, in a glass, not a paper cup, and with ice in it, and a little slice of lemon.
YOU STILL DON'T LIKE THE MAGICIAN, Huh?
I shook my head.
"WELL THAT'S OKAY. I SAID I'D SEE YOU BEFORE I WENT, DIDN'T I?"
I nodded.

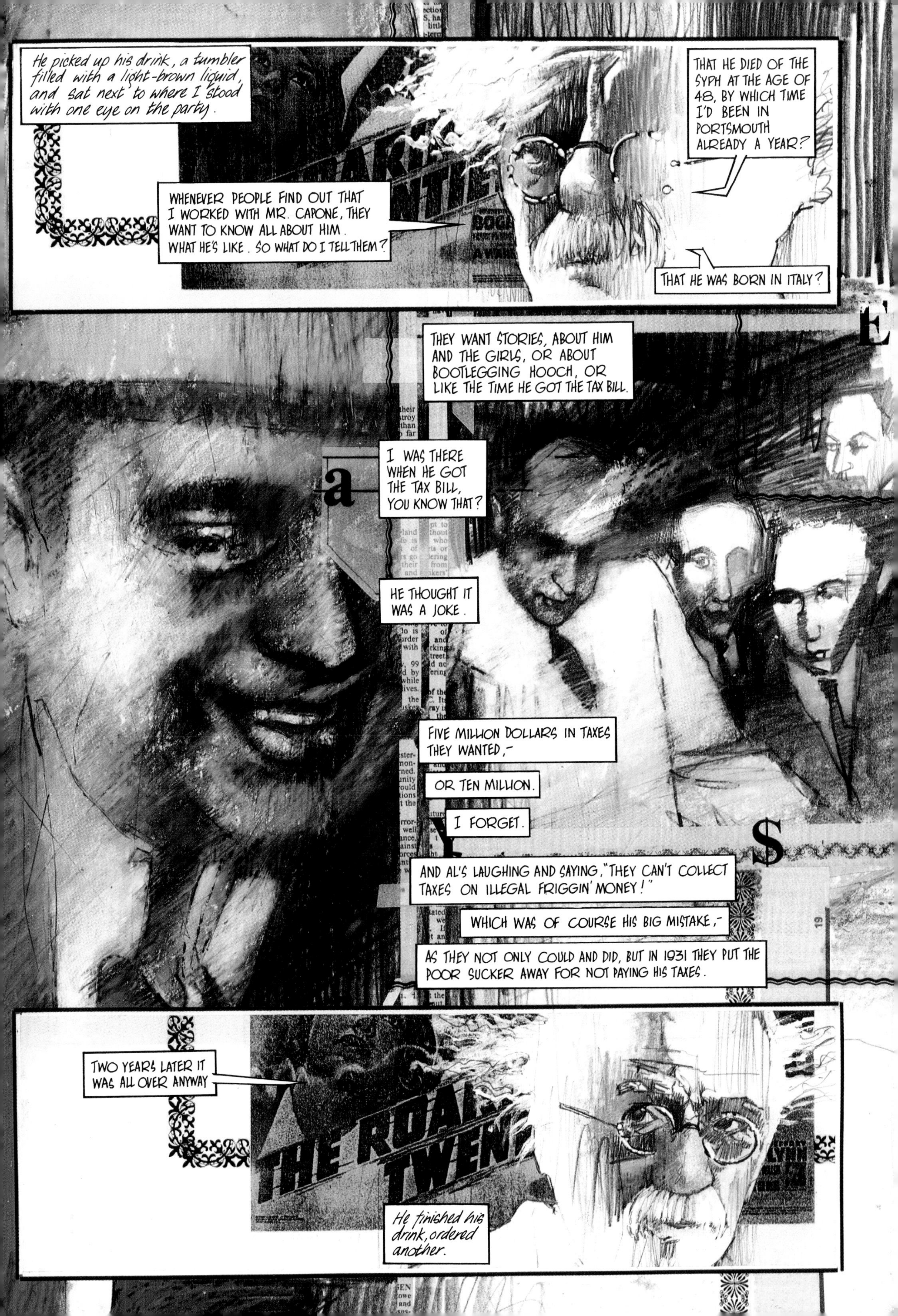
He picked up his drink, a tumbler filled with a light-brown liquid, and sat next to where I stood with one eye on the party.
WHENEVER PEOPLE FIND OUT THAT I WORKED WITH MR. CAPONE, THEY WANT TO KNOW ALL ABOUT HIM. WHAT HE'S LIKE. SO WHAT DO I TELL THEM?
THAT HE DIED OF THE SYPH AT THE AGE OF 48, BY WHICH TIME I'D BEEN IN PORTSMOUTH ALREADY A YEAR?
THAT HE WAS BORN IN ITALY?
THEY WANT STORIES, ABOUT HIM AND THE GIRLS, OR ABOUT BOOTLEGGING HOOCH, OR LIKE THE TIME HE GOT THE TAX BILL.
I WAS THERE WHEN HE GOT THE TAX BILL, YOU KNOW THAT?
HE THOUGHT IT WAS A JOKE.
FIVE MILLION DOLLARS IN TAXES THEY WANTED,-
OR TEN MILLION.
I FORGET.
AND AL'S LAUGHING AND SAYING, "THEY CAN'T COLLECT TAXES ON ILLEGAL FRIGGIN' MONEY!"
WHICH WAS OF COURSE HIS BIG MISTAKE,-
AS THEY NOT ONLY COULD AND DID, BUT IN 1931 THEY PUT THE POOR SUCKER AWAY FOR NOT PAYING HIS TAXES.
TWO YEARS LATER IT WAS ALL OVER ANYWAY
THE ROAR TWEN
He finished his drink, ordered another.

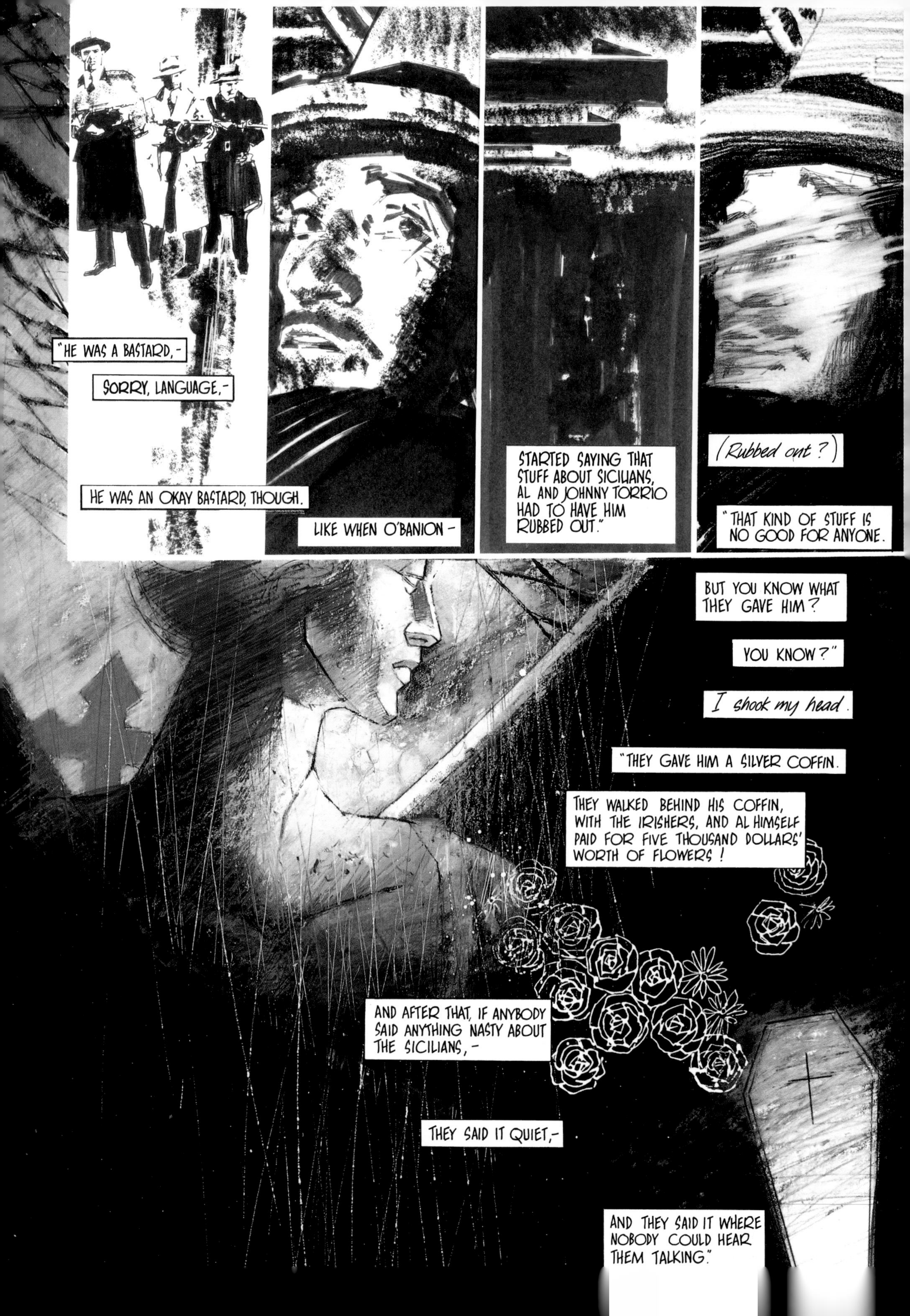
"HE WAS A BASTARD,-
SORRY, LANGUAGE,-
HE WAS AN OKAY BASTARD, THOUGH.
LIKE WHEN O'BANION -
STARTED SAYING THAT STUFF ABOUT SICILIANS, AL AND JOHNNY TORRIO HAD TO HAVE HIM RUBBED OUT."
(Rubbed out?)
"THAT KIND OF STUFF IS NO GOOD FOR ANYONE.
BUT YOU KNOW WHAT THEY GAVE HIM?
YOU KNOW?"
I shook my head.
"THEY GAVE HIM A SILVER COFFIN.
THEY WALKED BEHIND HIS COFFIN, WITH THE IRISHERS, AND AL HIMSELF PAID FOR FIVE THOUSAND DOLLARS' WORTH OF FLOWERS!
AND AFTER THAT, IF ANYBODY SAID ANYTHING NASTY ABOUT THE SICILIANS, -
THEY SAID IT QUIET,-
AND THEY SAID IT WHERE NOBODY COULD HEAR THEM TALKING."

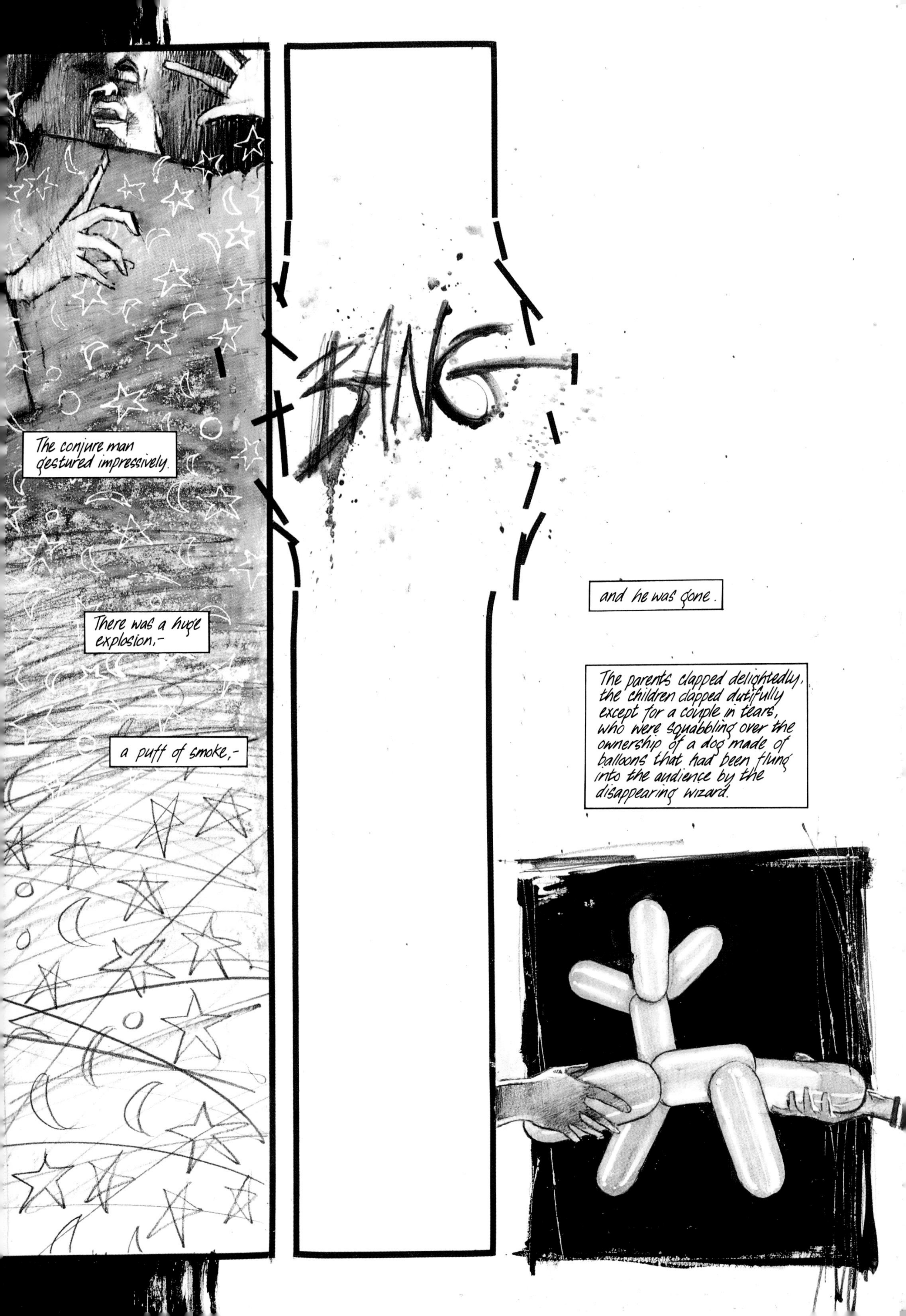
The conjure man gestured impressively.
There was a huge explosion,-
a puff of smoke,-
BANG
and he was gone.
The parents clapped delightedly, the children clapped dutifully except for a couple in tears, who were squabbling over the ownership of a dog made of balloons that had been flung into the audience by the disappearing wizard.

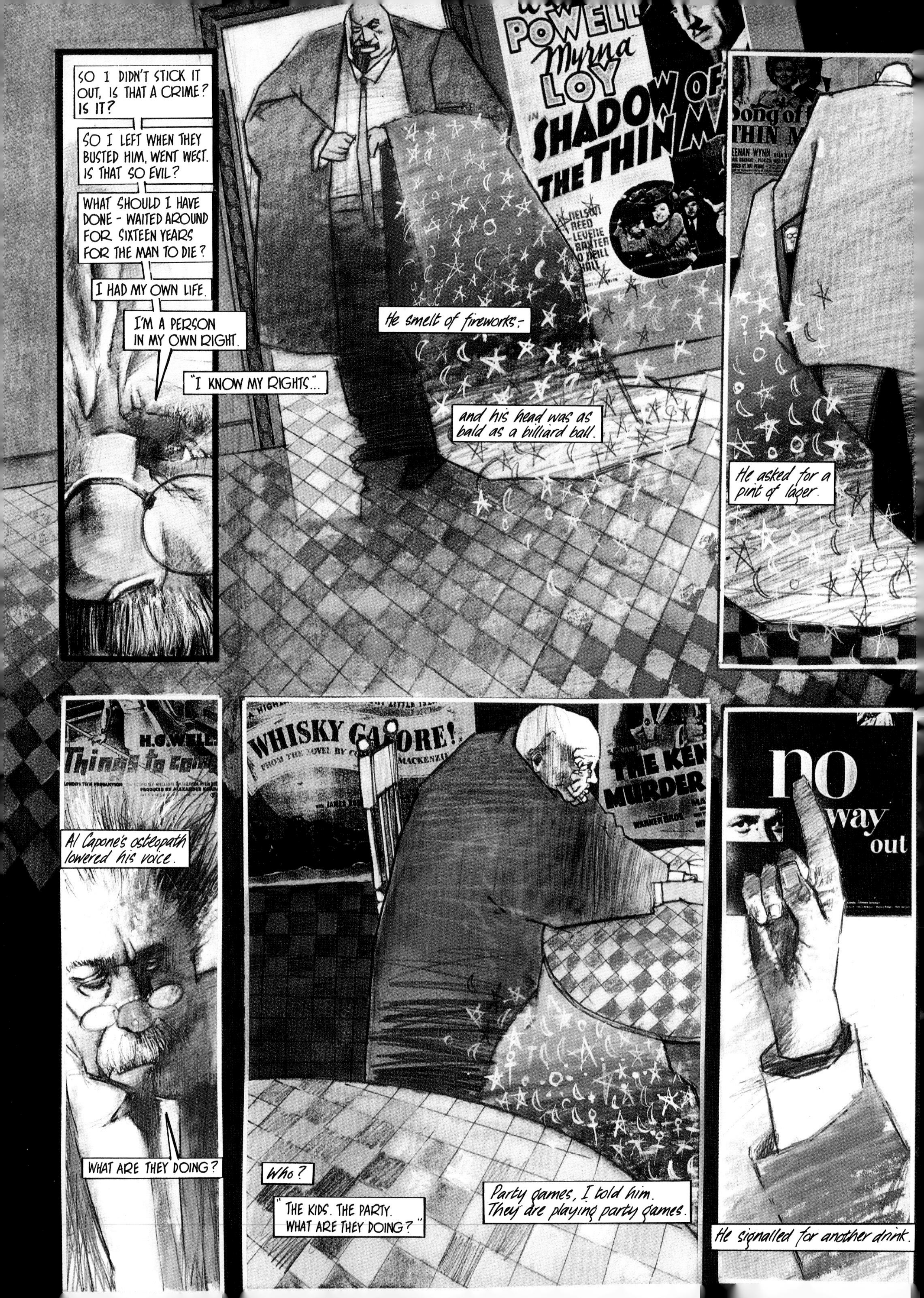

SO I DIDN'T STICK IT OUT, IS THAT A CRIME? IS IT?
SO I LEFT WHEN THEY BUSTED HIM, WENT WEST. IS THAT SO EVIL?
WHAT SHOULD I HAVE DONE - WAITED AROUND FOR SIXTEEN YEARS FOR THE MAN TO DIE?
I HAD MY OWN LIFE.
I'M A PERSON IN MY OWN RIGHT.
"I KNOW MY RIGHTS"...
POWELL
Myrna LOY
He smelt of fireworks:-
and his head was as bald as a billiard ball.
He asked for a pint of lager.
Al Capone's osteopath lowered his voice.
WHAT ARE THEY DOING?
Who?
"THE KIDS. THE PARTY. WHAT ARE THEY DOING?"
Party games, I told him. They are playing party games.
no
way
out
He signalled for another drink.

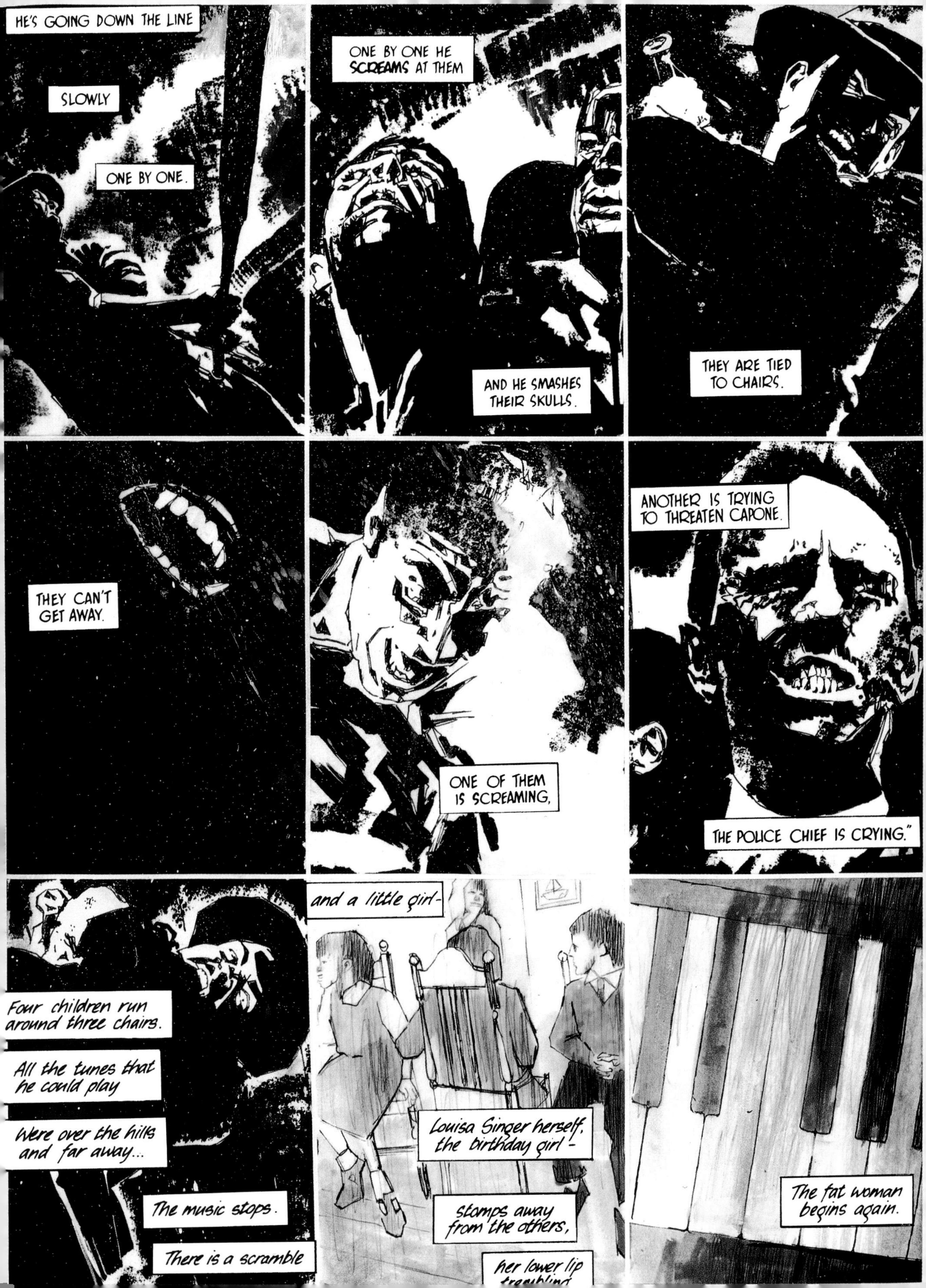
HE'S GOING DOWN THE LINE
SLOWLY
ONE BY ONE.
ONE BY ONE HE SCREAMS AT THEM
AND HE SMASHES THEIR SKULLS.
THEY ARE TIED TO CHAIRS.
THEY CAN'T GET AWAY.
ONE OF THEM IS SCREAMING,
ANOTHER IS TRYING TO THREATEN CAPONE.
THE POLICE CHIEF IS CRYING."
Four children run around three chairs.
All the tunes that he could play
Were over the hills and far away...
The music stops.
There is a scramble
and a little girl-
Louisa Singer herself, the birthday girl -
stomps away from the others,
her lower lip
The fat woman begins again.

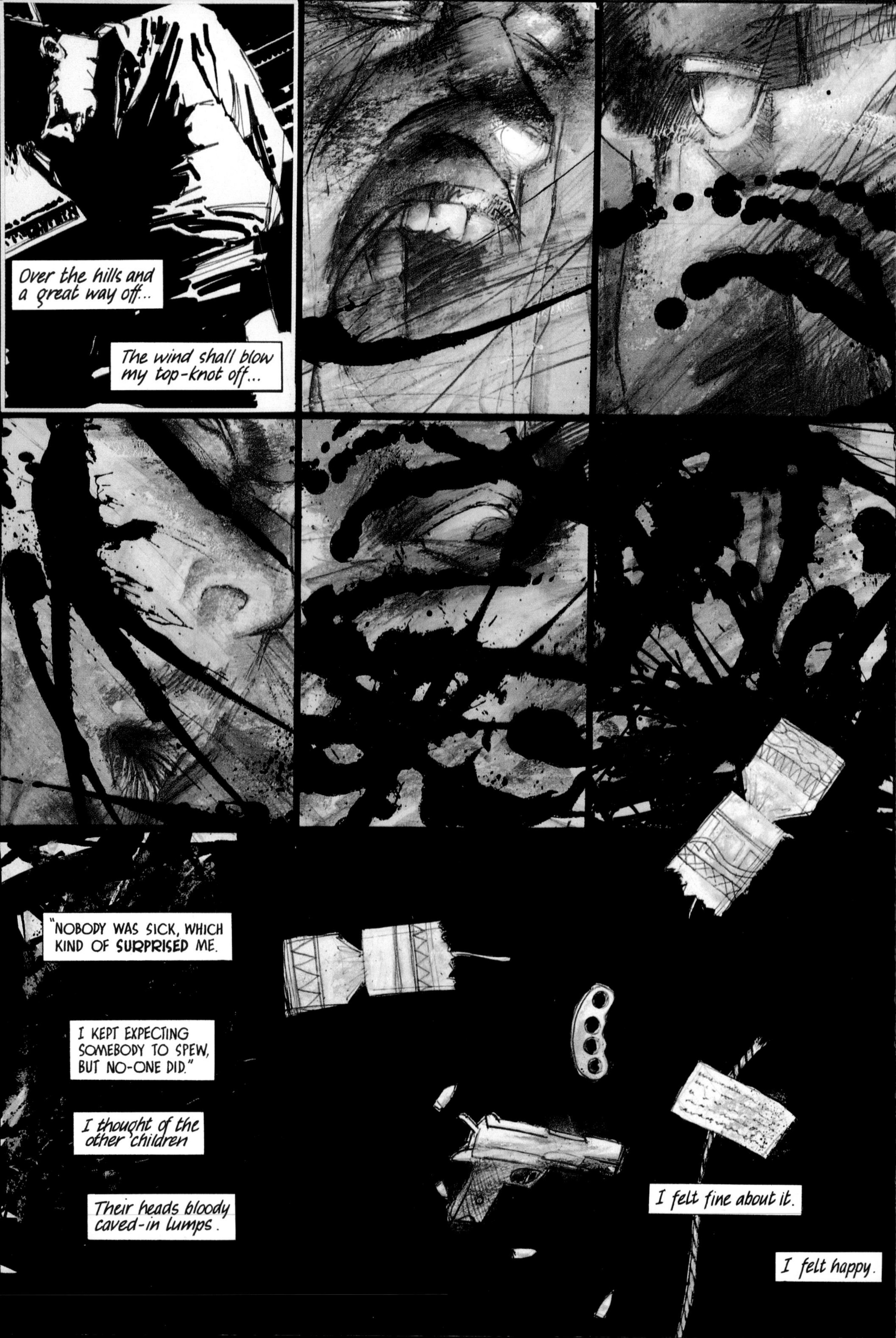
Over the hills and a great way off...
The wind shall blow my top-knot off...
"NOBODY WAS SICK, WHICH KIND OF SURPRISED ME.
I KEPT EXPECTING SOMEBODY TO SPEW, BUT NO-ONE DID."
I thought of the other children
Their heads bloody caved-in lumps.
I felt fine about it.
I felt happy.

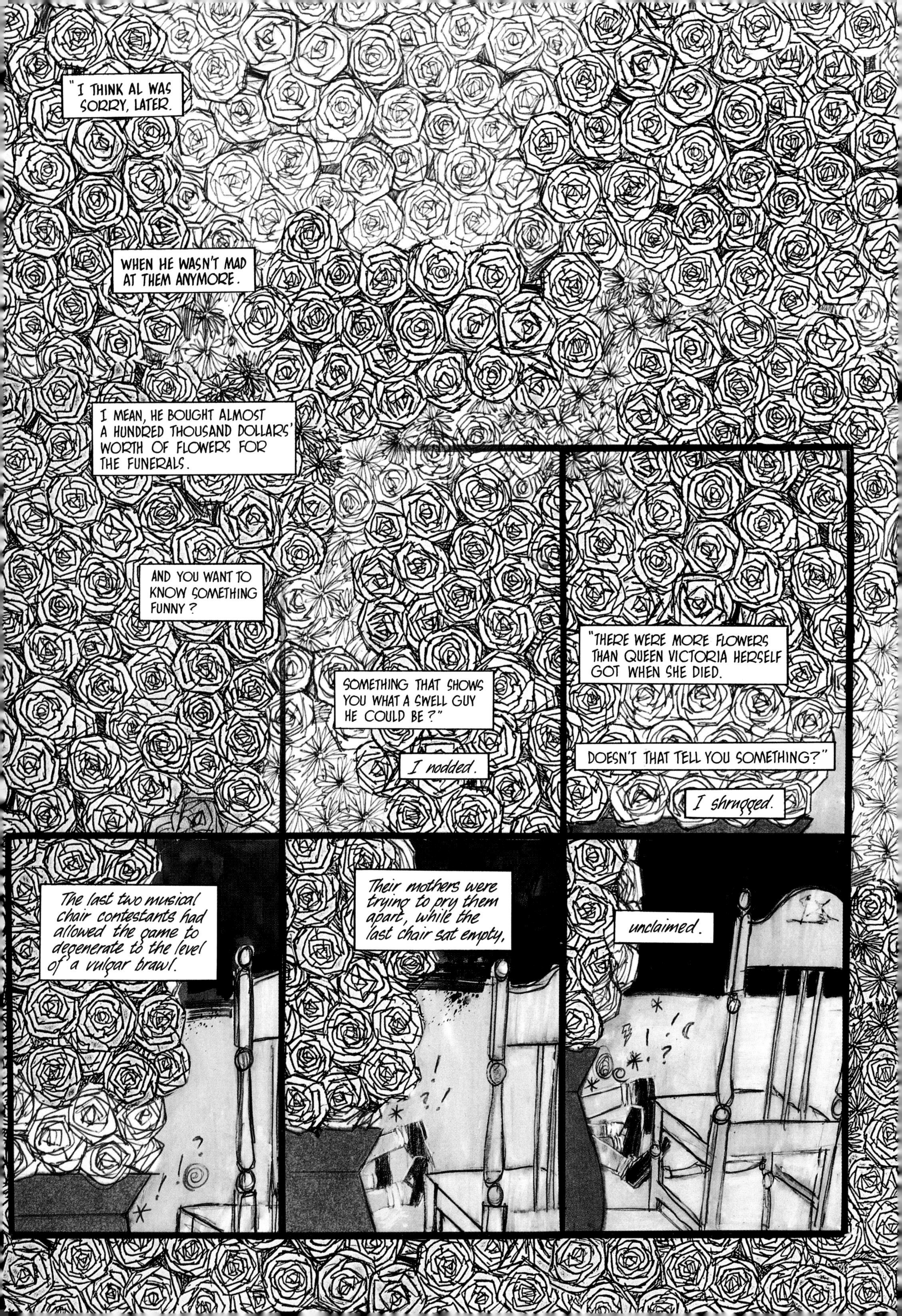
"I THINK AL WAS SORRY, LATER.
WHEN HE WASN'T MAD AT THEM ANYMORE.
I MEAN, HE BOUGHT ALMOST A HUNDRED THOUSAND DOLLARS' WORTH OF FLOWERS FOR THE FUNERALS.
AND YOU WANT TO KNOW SOMETHING FUNNY?
SOMETHING THAT SHOWS YOU WHAT A SWELL GUY HE COULD BE?"
I nodded.
"THERE WERE MORE FLOWERS THAN QUEEN VICTORIA HERSELF GOT WHEN SHE DIED.
DOESN'T THAT TELL YOU SOMETHING?"
I shrugged.
The last two musical chair contestants had allowed the game to degenerate to the level of a vulgar brawl.
Their mothers were trying to pry them apart, while the last chair sat empty,
unclaimed.

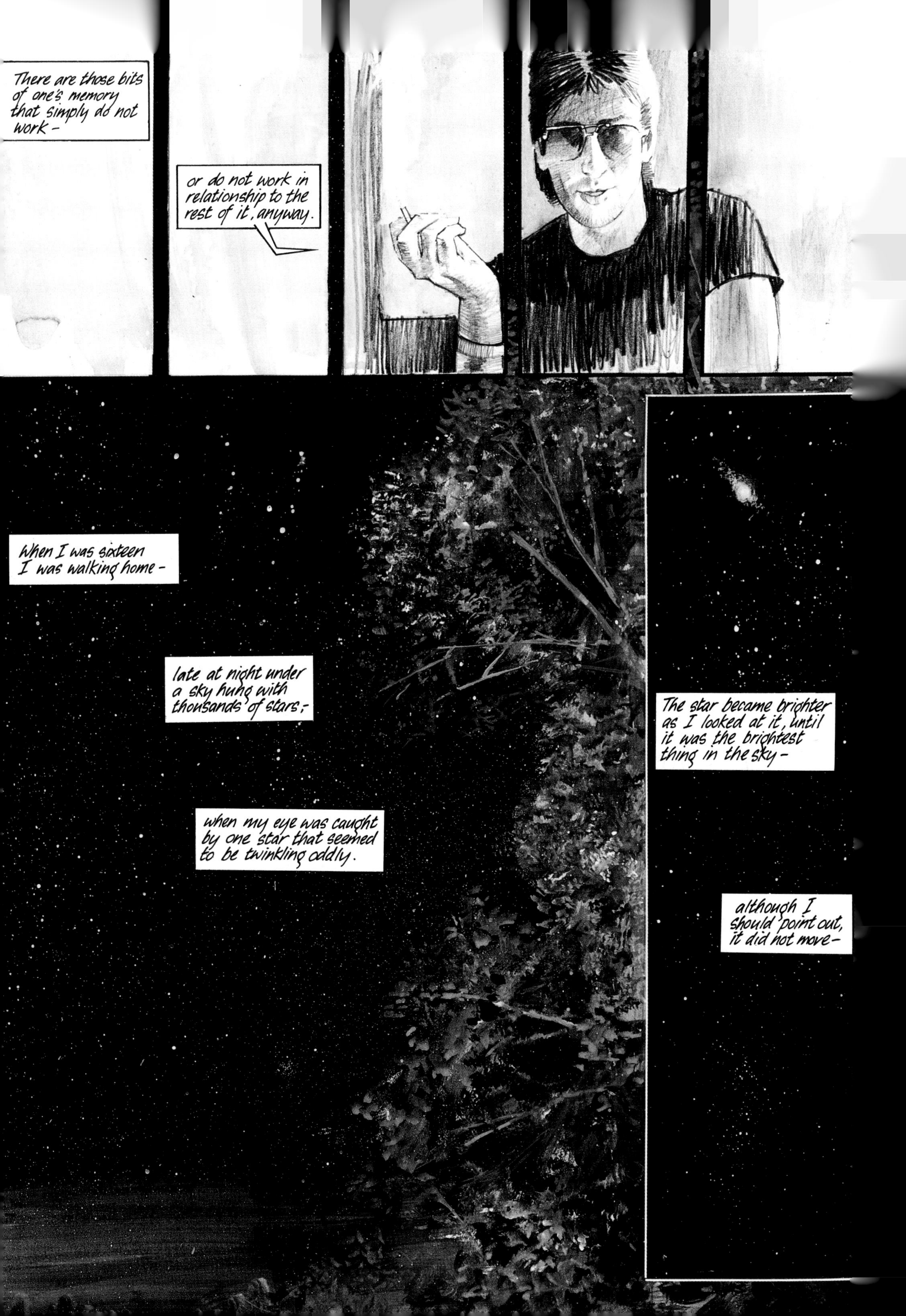
There are those bits of one's memory that simply do not work -
or do not work in relationship to the rest of it, anyway.
When I was sixteen I was walking home -
late at night under a sky hung with thousands of stars;-
when my eye was caught by one star that seemed to be twinkling oddly.
The star became brighter as I looked at it, until it was the brightest thing in the sky -
although I should point out, it did not move -

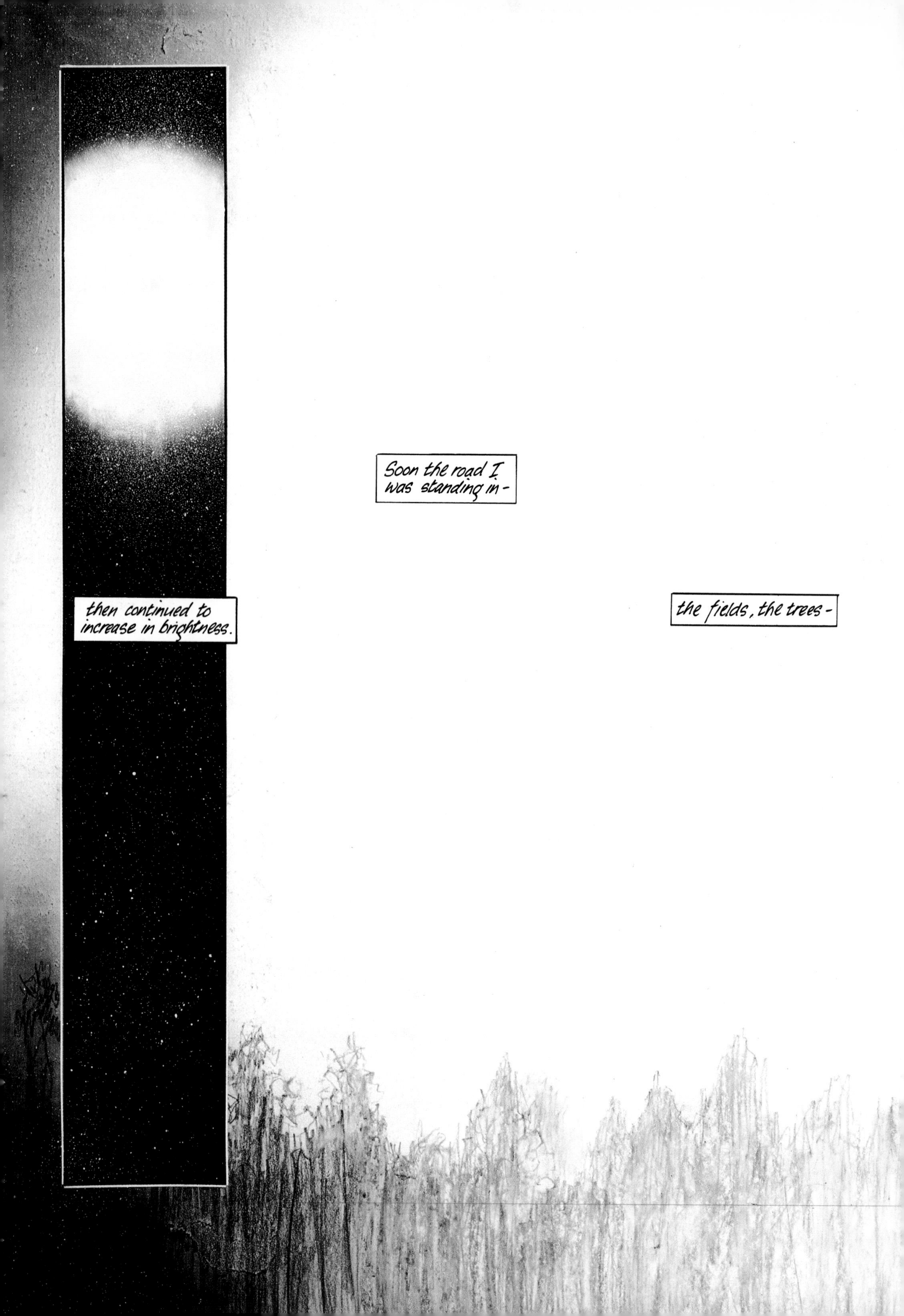
then continued to increase in brightness.
Soon the road I was standing in-
the fields, the trees-

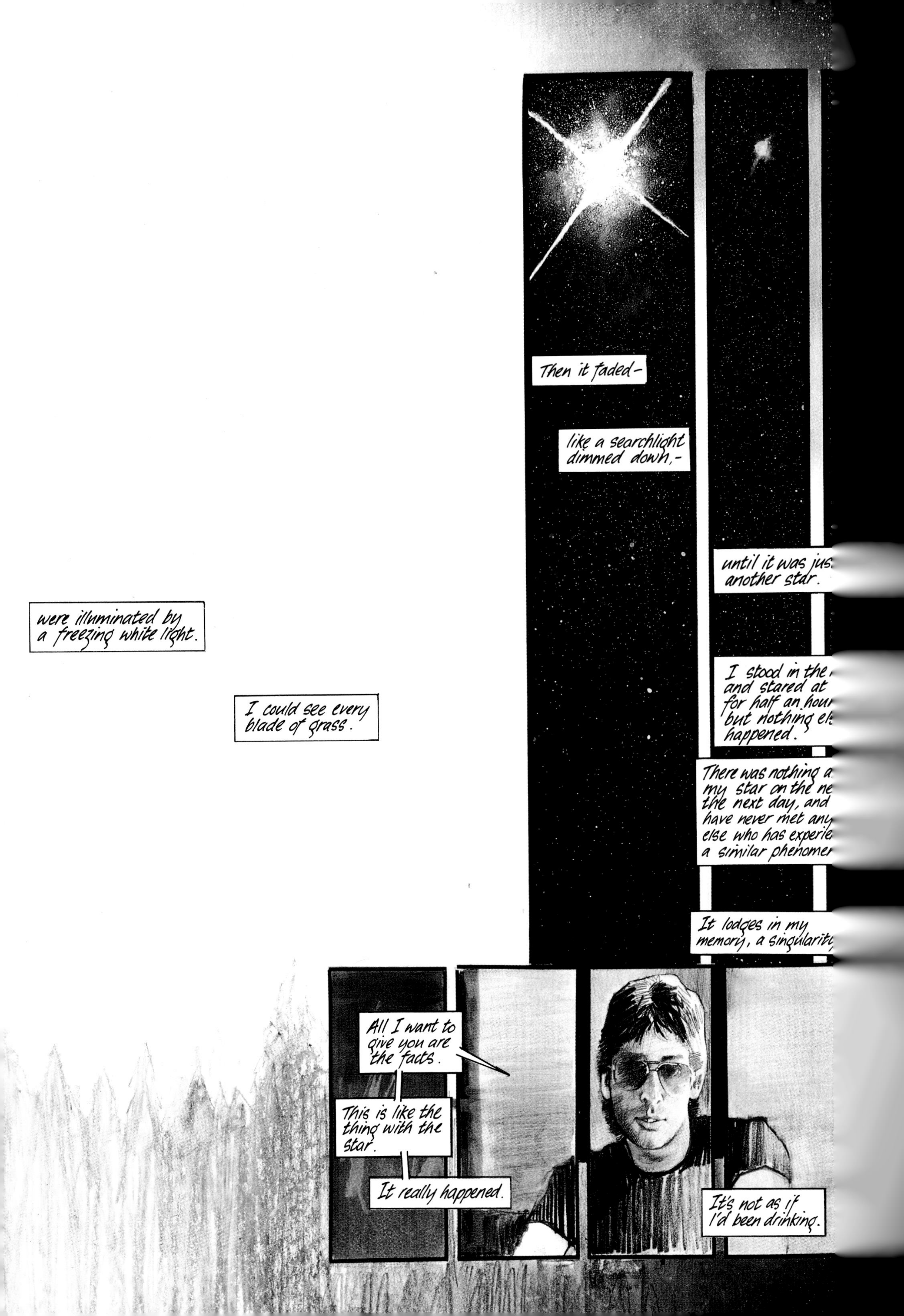
were illuminated by a freezing white light.
I could see every blade of grass.
Then it faded-
like a searchlight dimmed down,-
until it was jus another star.
I stood in the and stared at for half an hour but nothing el happened.
There was nothing a my star on the ne the next day, and have never met any else who has experie a similar phenome
It lodges in my memory, a singularity
All I want to give you are the facts.
This is like the thing with the star.
It really happened.
It's not as if I'd been drinking.

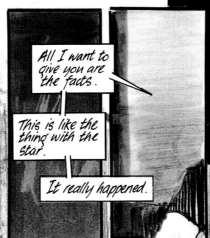

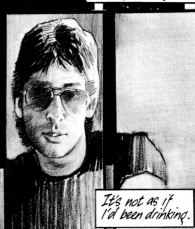

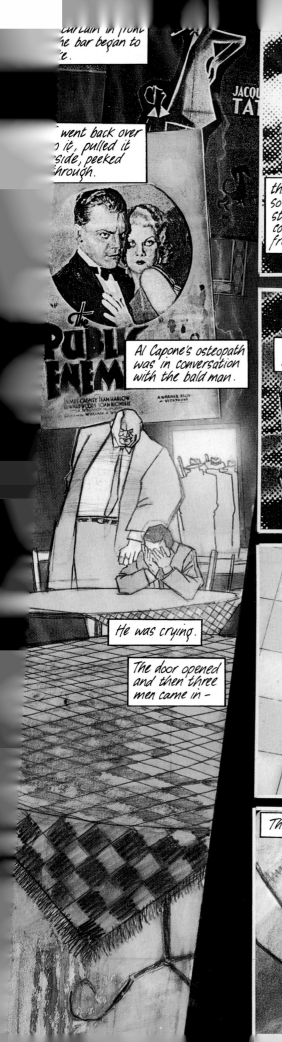

curtain in front
the bar began to
e.
went back over
o it, pulled it
side, peeked
hrough.
three men in suits so elegant and strange that I could hardly keep from crying out -
Al Capone's osteopath was in conversation with the bald man.
until I saw the menace in their eyes.
They carried baseball bats.
He was crying.
The door opened and then three men came in -
The conjuror saw them first.
He pulled a cigar from his breast pocket, put it in his mouth, and lit it.
Then he sat back in his chair.
The osteopath finished his drink.
ALFRED HITCHCOCK'S
THE MAN WHO KNEW TOO MUCH
The three men wore hats.

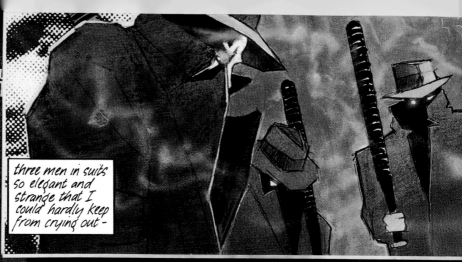

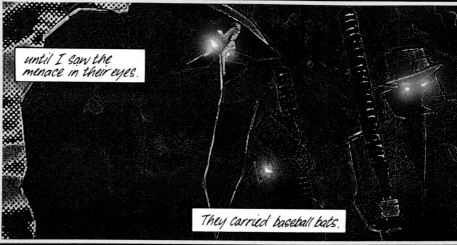

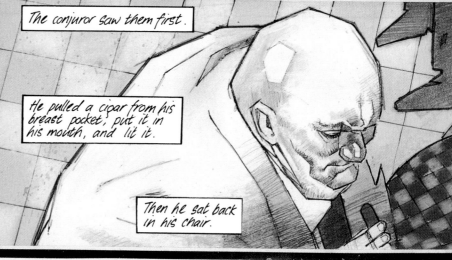

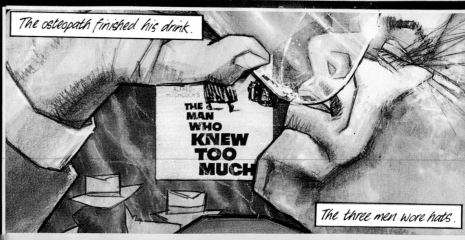

THEY DIED WITH THEIR BOOTS ON

ARTHUR KENNEDY · CHARLEY GRAPEWIN · GENE LOCKHART
A WARNER BROS. - FIRST NATIONAL PICTURE
Directed by RAOUL WALSH

...NEVE BEEN CALLING YOU FOR A LONG TIME

My osteopath stood up, –

reluctantly, –

and stood between the three.

The one who had spoken, spotted me peeping through the curtain at them; –

taller than the others, with a diamond glinting in a front tooth, –

he tipped his hat to me.

A STORY AS EXPLOSIVE AS HIS BLAZING AUTOMATICS

HUMPHREY BOGART
MARY ASTOR

The Maltese Falcon

DASHIELL HAMMETT
GEORGE · LORRE
JOHN HUSTON · WARNER BROS

I was delighted, and waved vigorously at all four of them until they were out of sight.

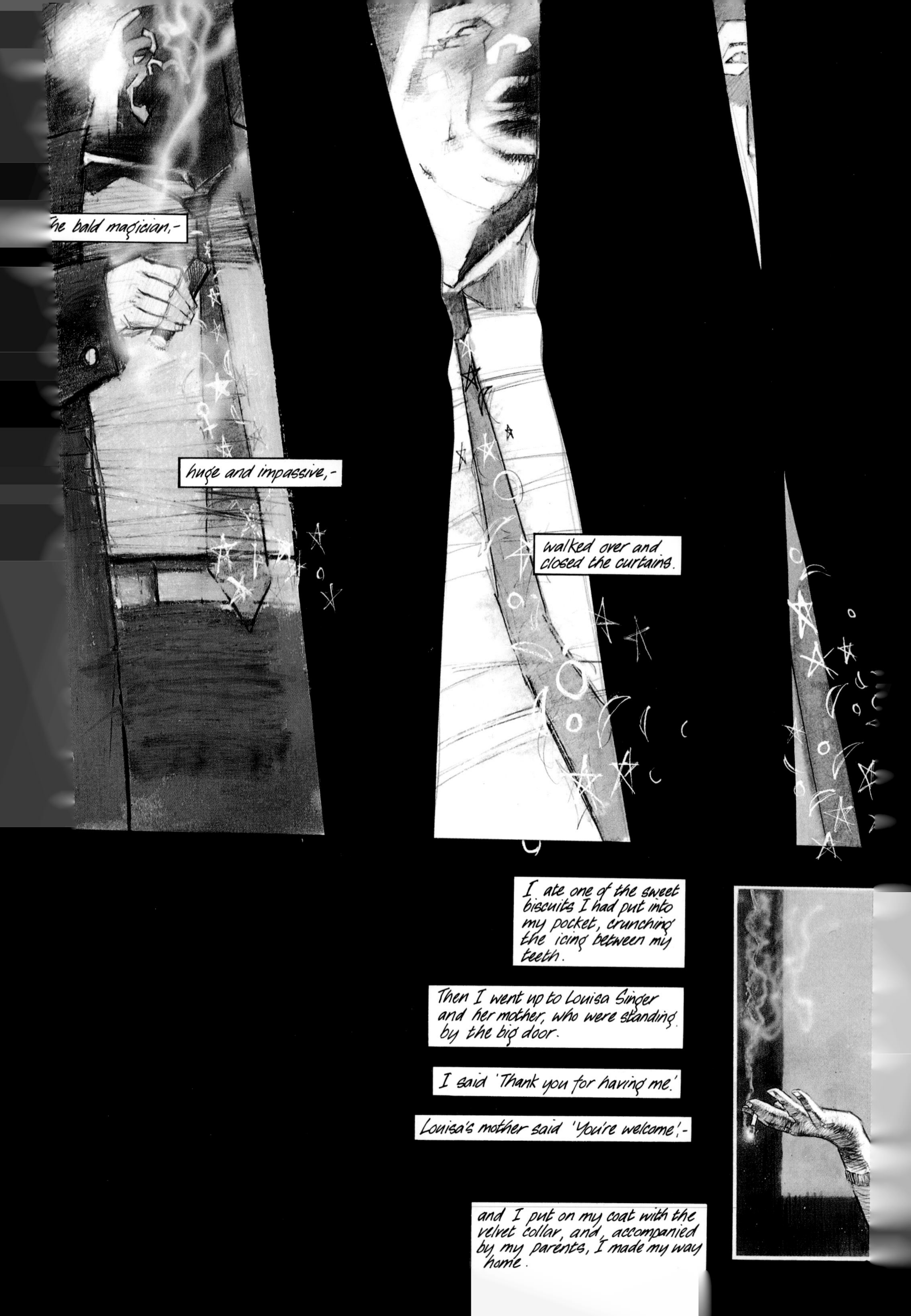
The bald magician,-
huge and impassive,-
walked over and closed the curtains.
I ate one of the sweet biscuits I had put into my pocket, crunching the icing between my teeth.
Then I went up to Louisa Singer and her mother, who were standing by the big door.
I said 'Thank you for having me.'
Louisa's mother said 'You're welcome',-
and I put on my coat with the velvet collar, and, accompanied by my parents, I made my way home.

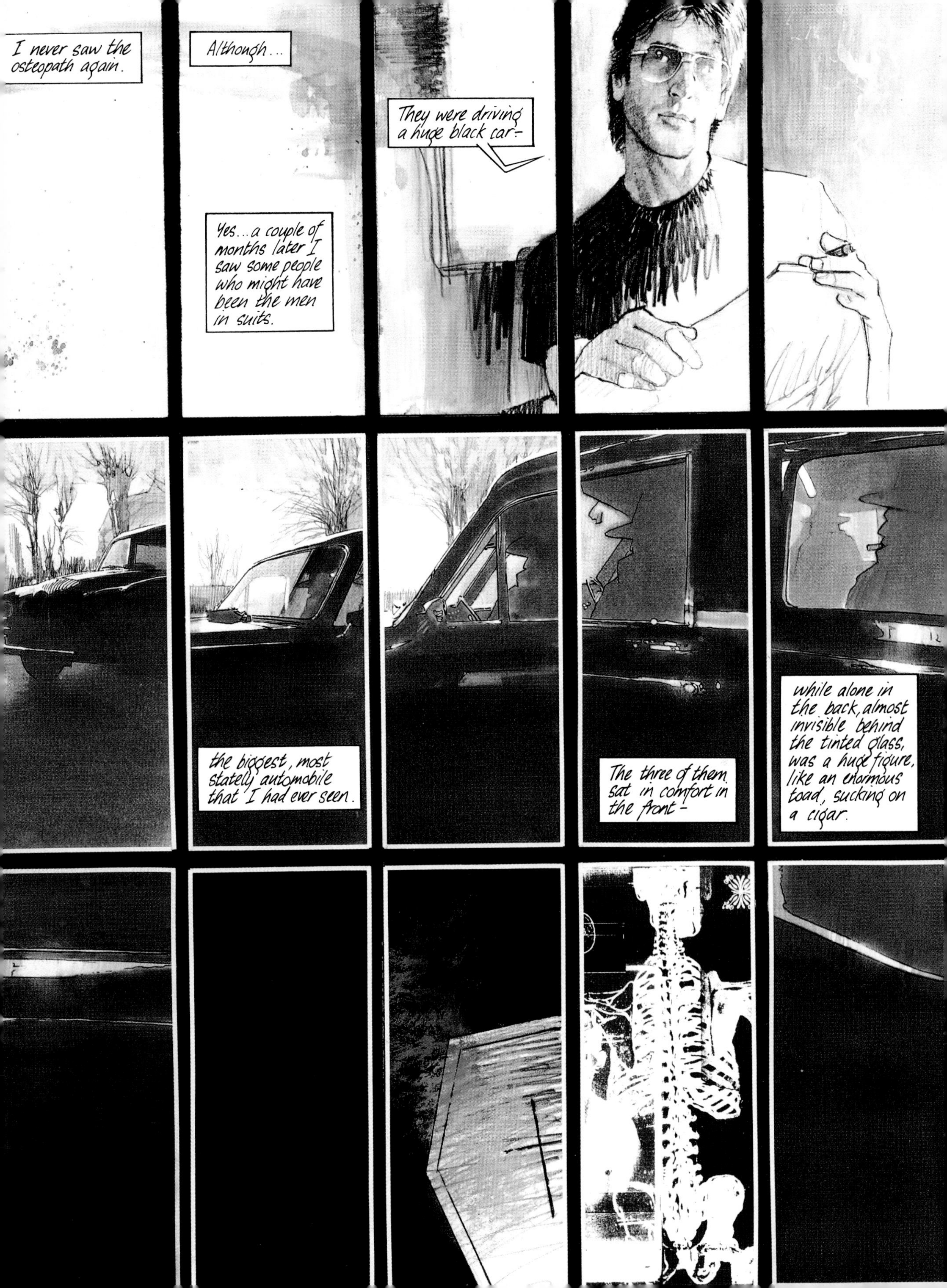
I never saw the osteopath again.
Although...
Yes... a couple of months later I saw some people who might have been the men in suits.
They were driving a huge black car-
the biggest, most stately automobile that I had ever seen.
The three of them sat in comfort in the front-
while alone in the back, almost invisible behind the tinted glass, was a huge figure, like an enormous toad, sucking on a cigar.

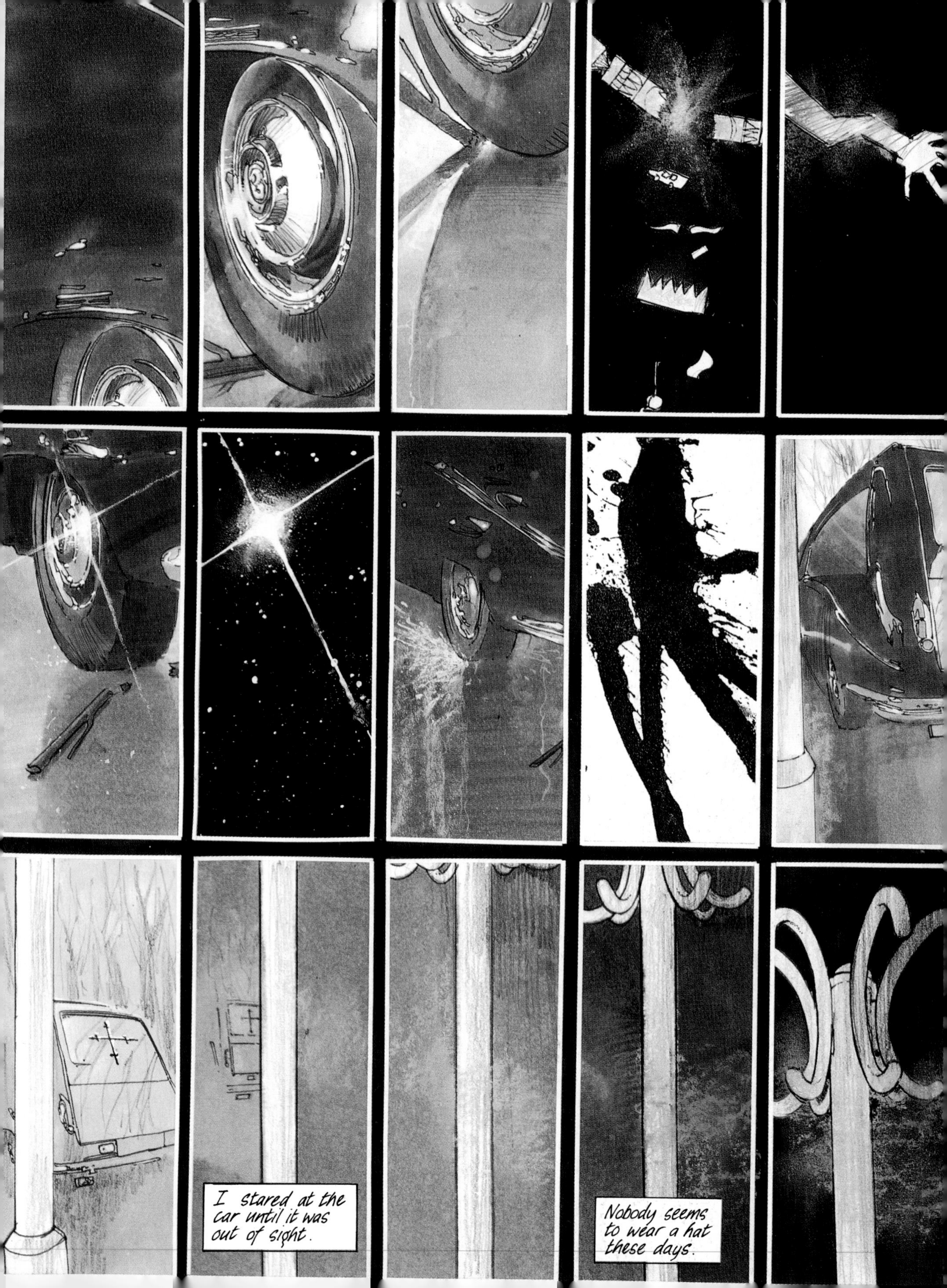
I stared at the car until it was out of sight.
Nobody seems to wear a hat these days.